~ WITNESSING HEAVEN ~

True Stories of Transformation from
Near-Death Experiences

A Love beyond Words

EDITORS OF GUIDEPOSTS

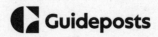

A Love beyond Words

Published by Guideposts Books & Inspirational Media
100 Reserve Road, Suite E200
Danbury, CT 06810
Guideposts.org

ACKNOWLEDGMENTS

Every attempt has been made to credit the sources of copyrighted material used in this book. If any such acknowledgment has been inadvertently omitted or miscredited, receipt of such information would be appreciated.

Scripture quotations marked (ESV) are taken from the *Holy Bible, English Standard Version*. Copyright © 2001 by Crossway Bibles, a division of Good News Publishers. Used by permission. All rights reserved.

Scripture quotations marked (GNT) are taken from the *Holy Bible, Good News Translation*. Copyright © 1992 by American Bible Society.

Scripture quotations marked (MSG) are taken from *The Message*. Copyright © 1993, 1994, 1995, 1996, 2000, 2001, 2002 by Eugene H. Peterson.

Scripture quotations marked (NIV) are taken from *The Holy Bible, New International Version*. Copyright © 1973, 1978, 1984, 2011 by Biblica, Inc. Used by permission of Zondervan. All rights reserved worldwide. zondervan.com

Scripture quotations marked (NLT) are from the *Holy Bible, New Living Translation*. Copyright © 1996, 2004, 2007 by Tyndale House Foundation. Used by permission of Tyndale House Publishers Inc., Carol Stream, Illinois. All rights reserved.

Scripture quotations marked (NRSV) are taken from the *New Revised Standard Version Bible*. Copyright © 1989 by the Division of Christian Education of the National Council of the Churches of Christ in the United States of America. Used by permission. All rights reserved.

Cover design by Pamela Walker, W Design Studio
Interior design by Pamela Walker, W Design Studio
Cover photo by Dreamstime
Typeset by Aptara, Inc.

Printed and bound in the United States of America
10 9 8 7 6 5 4 3 2 1

Do not conform to the pattern of this world, but be transformed by the renewing of your mind. Then you will be able to test and approve what God's will is—his good, pleasing and perfect will.

Romans 12:2 (NIV)

CONTENTS

INTRODUCTION

But God demonstrates his own love for us in this:
While we were still sinners, Christ died for us.

Romans 5:8 (NIV)

God is love. Just three short words with mind-blowing implications. Yet it can be easy to become desensitized toward them and forget just how powerful they really are. Knowing them is one thing; fully understanding and embracing them is another, and we can easily spend a lifetime and still not fully grasp their full import.

The reality is that no words—no matter how eloquent and lofty they might be—can fully capture the essence of God's amazing love for us. In fact, for each of the people featured in this volume, it took something *beyond* words, beyond life itself for them to "have the power to understand, as all God's people should, how wide, how long, how high, and how deep his love is" (Ephesians 3:18, NLT). And even then, as you'll read in these and many stories of near-death experiences, those who have witnessed heaven struggle to find the words to describe the love they felt during their NDEs.

Light that is so incredibly bright, yet it doesn't hurt the eyes of those who see it. Music that flows not only to the ears but also in and through the listeners, inviting them to join in the song. Colors that are identifiable but somehow brighter, deeper, richer, and more vibrant than any color seen in this earthy life. And an all-encompassing, all-knowing love that envelops them like a warm embrace.

As you read the captivating stories in this volume, it is our hope and prayer that when you turn the last page and close the book, you'll have just a little deeper understanding of God's indescribable love for you.

Love: Heaven's Magnificent Promise

By Jeffrey Long, MD

*So we have come to know and to believe the love that
God has for us. God is love, and whoever abides in
love abides in God, and God abides in him.*

1 John 4:16 (ESV)

Passages about love are among the most beautiful and inspirational in the Bible because love fascinates us more than just about anything. This is not surprising, as throughout our lives the love we show others is among the most important expressions of our faith.

I am a physician practicing the medical specialty of radiation oncology, which is the use of radiation to treat cancer. Over twenty years ago, I began studying near-death experiences (NDEs) using the best scientific methods available. For this investigation, I developed the Near-Death Experience Research Foundation (NDERF, nderf.org) with a website that allows people to share narratives of their experiences and to answer a detailed survey. Currently, there are over one hundred survey questions. This allowed NDE research to reach an entirely new level, in which we are discovering more about the details and meanings of NDEs than was ever possible before.

As I write this, there are sections of the NDERF website in over thirty different languages allowing people from all over the world to share their near-death experiences. Over 4,000 NDEs have been shared with NDERF and are posted on the nderf.org website. To my knowledge,

> *NDE-ers almost always report that their NDEs were vastly different from dreams.*

this is by far the largest collection of NDEs publicly available in the world. Having so many NDEs to study is crucial as we can be more confident than ever of the groundbreaking findings from investigating them. My NDE research was published in a *New York Times* best-selling book with nine lines of evidence that established the reality of NDEs.[1] As remarkable as NDEs often seem, it is important to remember that virtually all near-death experiencers (NDE-ers) believed their experiences to be absolutely real. NDE-ers almost always report that their NDEs were vastly different from dreams or any other state of altered consciousness.

Near-Death Experience Overview

As a physician and scientist, I am cautious about using the term "miracle." However, there seems no better word to describe near-death experiences. NDE-ers are so severely physically compromised that they are generally unconscious at the time of the experience, or even clinically dead without a heartbeat. By the dictionary definition of *unconscious*, it should be impossible to have a lucid detailed experience. And yet that is what many thousands of NDE-ers report.

NDEs are not especially rare. A Gallup poll found that about 5 percent of those surveyed affirmed they had an NDE at some time during their lives.[2] At the time of a life-threatening event, about 17 percent will have an NDE.[3] We cannot predict who will and will not have an NDE during a close brush with death.[4] NDEs happen to children and adults. They happen to people from every walk of life, including ministers and priests. During an NDE, there is a consistent pattern of features that may occur such as a tunnel, unearthly light, intense and positive emotions, an encounter with deceased loved ones, awareness of their prior life, and a visit to a heavenly realm.

Among the most remarkable findings of investigating near-death experiences are insights about *love*. As we talk about the love that NDE-ers describe, you may find yourself smiling in realization that such powerful and all-encompassing insights about love are seen over and over in the Bible.

Christian Love

Everyone I know likes to think about love. Hearing and thinking about love can be beautifully inspirational and comforting. It's no wonder that church sermons talking about love are so popular!

We should keep in mind that Christian love is an *exceptional* kind of love. I am in complete agreement with Alexander Strauch, a teacher of philosophy and New Testament literature at Colorado Christian University, when he says: "Christian love is never theoretical or abstract; it is always practical."[5]

Christians understand that love is their faith in *action*. Christian love can flow from the awareness of how much God loves them. In my research about love in near-death experiences I concluded *that* "God loves us regardless of who we are, what we look like, how young or old we are, or what our shortcomings may be. We are loved by God for exactly who we are and what we are."[6]

Jay E. Adams, who received his doctorate in preaching and has written over one hundred books, shares his wisdom in all of his writings. Among the treasure trove of insights was what he had to say about Christian love:

> Love at first is not feeling. Love first can be expressed as giving. That is at the core of love. If one gives, the feeling of love will follow. To love we must give of ourselves, of our time, of our substance, of whatever it takes to show love; for giving is fundamental to the Biblical idea of love.[7]

This same concept of Christian love was shared by C. S. Lewis, one of the great Christian theologians. He was a faculty member at both Oxford University and Cambridge University. Lewis talks about the vital issue of relationships and Christian love in his classic book *Mere Christianity*:

> Love as distinct from "being in love" is not merely a feeling. It is a deep unity, maintained by the will and deliberately strengthened by habit; reinforced by the grace which both partners ask, and receive from God. They can have this love for each other even at those moments when they do not like each other; as you love yourself even when you do not like yourself.[8]

It's not surprising that one of the most famous verses in the Bible talks about love. I always have a smile on my face when I read 1 Corinthians 13:4–6 (ESV):

> Love is patient and kind; love does not envy or boast; it is not arrogant or rude. It does not insist on its own way; it is not irritable or resentful; it does not rejoice at wrongdoing, but rejoices with the truth.

Just a few verses later, 1 Corinthians 13:13 reminds us how important love is:

> So now faith, hope, and love abide, these three; but the greatest of these is love.

There is a great deal to learn about love in the Bible. Every turn of the page seems to bring up yet another glorious insight about love. The word *love* is used 552 times in 506 verses in the Bible.[9] Love is also one of the most commonly used words in near-death experiences.

Envisioning God's perfect love reminds us that in our earthly lives love often seems far away. Our lives may seem like an ongoing struggle through trials and tribulations. How can we manifest God's love in the world when our lives are often so challenging? We are heartened by our Christian understanding that we can turn to God at any time. Biblical concepts about love can be relevant to *everything* we encounter in life. God's love for us never diminishes and is always with us in both good and difficult times. We won't be perfect as we seek to be as loving as we can be, but God knows that. As long as we do our best to be loving, I am sure that we are growing closer to God.

Love in Heaven

We love because he first loved us.

1 John 4:19 (ESV)

Near-death experiencers often describe visiting unearthly realms so breathtaking and majestic that they could reasonably be called heavenly. These realms are remarkably different from what we experience in our everyday lives. By the hundreds, NDE-ers have reported landscapes analogous to those on earth,

Near-death experiencers often describe visiting unearthly realms remarkably different from what we experience in our everyday lives.

but with a loveliness and vibrancy that often goes beyond earthly language. They may encounter colors and music that are beautiful beyond anything possible on earth. They may see splendid buildings. They frequently have joyous reunions with their deceased loved ones who appear in picture-perfect health. A magnificent and unearthly light may be present. And, of course, they have a sense of enormous love.

In his near-death experience shared with NDERF, Peter encountered overwhelming love when he had an NDE as the result of a severe motorbike accident (paraphrased below for clarity):

There was light as far as I was able to see. I knew that beyond what I could see there was the light. The light did not hurt my vision, even though it was very bright. This light was beyond description in its extent, range, and magnitude. The unique characteristic of this light was that of absolute love. The light's love was totally free of reservation; it was limitless and infinite. The love I encountered possessed a personality that I could feel with my every fiber as it flowed into me, through me, and touched every single part of me. There was no part of me untouched by this love. I was utterly and completely permeated by this love. I never had a sensation on earth that in any way comes close to what this being extended to me freely and without reservation. This being and light was complete love. I was immersed and permeated by the intelligence and wisdom of this being while in that total love. The indescribable intelligence and wisdom of this being and light was infinite.... As I try (and fail) to write about the un-writeable, I must drop the pen and say that this being was awesome in the extent of its power, magnitude, and beauty. No words can describe the magnitude of the magnificence of this being. All that this being was capable of, what it did, and what it gave could be summarized as its one essential quality: It was sheer, unalloyed, and absolute love.[10]

There have been hundreds of near-death experience accounts reporting a love that is consistently described as far beyond anything the experiencers ever encountered in their lives and often indescribable with earthly words. Here are examples of what those who had NDEs learned about love during their experiences:

The paramount element of reality.[11]

I knew the being I met was composed in its very atoms of a substance I can only call love. Love is the only word I have.[12]

I knew that love was the greatest force around us and that we are all love and love is the only thing that is real, that hatred and pain and hurt and all the negative things were not really the way it is. It's just that we create these negative thoughts.[13]

Love was everywhere. It permeated the afterlife. It was incredible.[14]

I was loved unconditionally despite my faults and fears.[15]

To overcome our fears, we need to love and accept ourselves and each other. The actions and choices we make can either be from love or fear—love is golden light, fear is darkness.[16]

The love I felt was unique. I felt utterly safe that nothing could happen. My pain ceased. All of my worries and fears that I previously had were left behind with my body. Only a few can get an idea of what this love is like.[17]

Love is All That Is, in a sense. The word "love" is only the closest word we have—it's not really accurate but I can't do any better with our language.[18]

I could go on quoting from near-death experiencers, but I am sure you see the pattern. I am always amazed at the remarkable similarity between descriptions of love in the Bible and the love encountered during NDEs.

Love of God

Beloved, let us love one another, for love is from God,
and whoever loves has been born of God and knows God.

1 John 4:7 (ESV)

Have you ever wondered what it would be like to meet God in heaven? This fascinating question led me to study 144 near-death experiences from people who described an encounter with God or awareness of Him during their NDEs.[19] NDE-ers who encountered God often describe God's love.

The love of God in a near-death experience is well expressed by a woman named Veronica. Veronica wasn't sure if it was the stings from wasps or hornets that led to her close brush with death, but she is certain that she went into shock and had an NDE:

> *Have you ever wondered what it would be like to meet God in heaven? NDE-ers who encountered God often describe God's love.*

The most emotionally powerful and heartbreakingly beautiful instant was sensing God's love for me. My human vision was obscured by a great light which was soft and part of God's love. The appearance of God and the other spiritual beings was as translucent outlines of white or light, but I could not see details. Everything was focused in a spiritual manner on love and information. My feelings of love and thankfulness toward God was and is overpowering and supremely beautiful beyond measure. I felt fearless, which was strange because I am often anxious in my earthly life. I never before felt so safe, known, loved, understood, and cared for. I was euphoric and yet calm. I wanted to stay there immersed in God's love. I needed to be reminded of those on earth that I love, because heaven's love was so inviting. God is perfect, complete, and highly evolved love. Yet God has a soul and identity. I sensed that we are all on a path to that love and God. The foremost purpose is love and realizing the source, which is God. What can become is profoundly beautiful and right. All others count, including nature and precious animals. Our purpose and goal is God's perfect love and to continually learn and serve God. We must love, serve others, love ourselves, and grow spiritually. We all must understand God's love.[20]

In many near-death experiences, God's love is generally described as all-encompassing and completely accepting of NDE-ers for who they are and everything they are. Even atheists have reported NDEs where they encountered God. As you would expect, many atheists cease to be atheists after such an experience.

> *In many near-death experiences, God's love is described as all-encompassing.*

Ultimate love is God and flows from God. The Bible shares many inspiring and informative passages about God's love. In 2 Timothy 1:7 (ESV) we find this concept beautifully expressed:

For God gave us a spirit not of fear but of power and love and self-control.

One of the most essential things for all of humanity to know about God is that *God is love*. Imagine what a better world this would be if everyone understood this! As we share our Christian love with others, there may be times when we forget how valuable our expressions of love are. The next time you perform a loving act, consider that you are acting as God's representative on earth. Your loving action is, in a very real way, your connection with God as you share God's love with others. No act of love is too small to matter. All that is love matters to God.

We love God because God first loved us. We can never love God perfectly, but God understands this. The Bible shares some important passages to keep in mind as we reflect on loving God, such as Romans 8:28 (ESV): "We know that for those who love God all things work together for good, for those who are called according to his purpose."

For those who love God, He is at work in their lives as part of His purpose. An essential concept about love is *connection*, in that we connect with what we love. As we align our lives ever closer to God, our bond grows, and we are never alone.

Perhaps the greatest expression of God's love for us was His gift of Jesus. As it says in John 3:16 (ESV), one of the most widely quoted verses of the Bible: "For God so loved the world, that he gave his only Son, that whoever believes in him should not perish but have eternal life."

In the New Testament, Jesus shares many valuable teachings about love. These vital lessons about love have been an inspiration for over two thousand years and continue to inspire us today.

Love of Jesus

A new commandment I give to you, that you love one another:
just as I have loved you, you also are to love one another.
John 13:34 (ESV)

Encounters with Jesus are described in many near-death experiences. These encounters are among the most inspiring part of what NDE-ers experienced. Even the word *inspiring* seems too mild for the awesome sense of love, peace, and joy NDE-ers commonly describe when they encounter Jesus.

To say that NDE-er Carolyn nearly died seems like an understatement. Carolyn had a near-death experience when her bowels burst, her lungs collapsed, and her kidneys failed. She recovered but later said: "After consultations with my surgeons, they have admitted that it is not medically possible that I am alive." During her NDE, Carolyn encountered Jesus:

> *He was looking toward me with enormous compassion and love. His eyes revealed a purity, holiness, and emotion beyond human ability.*

I had no body. I saw a man dressed in a brilliant white robe. His clothes were bright like a lightning bolt. He drenched me in total euphoria as He radiated light and love. His love for me was engulfing as I looked at Him in absolute awe. It was like being in an ocean where water is rushing inside and outside of you. My every cell was soaked in His love to absolute saturation. He walked toward me holding the hand of a young girl. I knew the little girl was me. Suddenly I was within the little girl and saw through her eyes. As I turned my head, I looked up at Him. He was looking down toward me with enormous compassion and love. His eyes revealed a purity, holiness, and emotion that was beyond human ability. I knew that no human could feel even a speck of His enormous love. He loved me, and I was His child. He then spoke to me through thought and not with words, saying, "It's not your time yet."[21]

The Bible shares valuable insights about love from Mary, who anointed Jesus's feet in Bethany at a dinner. John 12:1–8 (ESV) shares this remarkable story:

> Six days before the Passover, Jesus therefore came to Bethany, where Lazarus was, whom Jesus had raised from the dead. So they gave a dinner for him there. Martha served, and Lazarus was one of those reclining with him at table. Mary therefore took a pound of expensive ointment made from pure nard, and anointed the feet of Jesus and wiped his feet with her hair. The house was filled with the fragrance of the perfume. But Judas Iscariot, one of his disciples (he who was about to betray him), said, "Why was this ointment not sold for three hundred denarii and given to the poor?" He said this, not because he cared about the poor, but because he was a thief, and having charge of the moneybag he used to help himself to what was put into it. Jesus said, "Leave her alone, so that she may keep it for the day of my burial. For the poor you always have with you, but you do not always have me."

The ointment used by Mary was exceptionally expensive. Its value of three hundred denarii was about what a common laborer earned in a year. But when it came to Mary showing her love for Jesus, the cost of the ointment didn't matter. We know from the Bible that Mary's love for Jesus was as pure as her precious ointment. Love this profound is unconditional and gives everything. Romans 8:39 (ESV, adapted) further shows the limitless love of Jesus:

> Neither height nor depth, nor anything else in all creation, will be able to separate us from the love of God in Christ Jesus our Lord.

God's love is for all of us, at all times and wherever we are. It is pure and perfect. You can see that the love described in the Bible and encountered in NDEs is often so profound and encompassing that words can hardly do it justice.

> *God's love is for all of us, at all times and wherever we are.*

With each turn of the page of *A Love beyond Words,* may you feel a great sense of inspiration, reassurance, and peace. These are among the most important understandings of the NDEs shared here.

References

1. Jeffrey Long, Paul Perry, *Evidence of the Afterlife: The Science of Near-Death Experiences* (New York, NY: HarperCollins), 2010.
2. George Gallup Jr., William Proctor, *Adventures in Immortality: A Look Beyond the Threshold of Death* (New York: McGraw-Hill, 1982).
3. Nancy Zingrone, Carlos Alvarado, "Pleasurable Western Adult Near-Death Experiences: Features, Circumstances, and Incidence,"

in Janice Holden, Bruce Greyson, Debbie James, editors, *The Handbook of Near-Death Experiences: Thirty Years of Investigation* (Santa Barbara, CA: Praeger/ABC-CLIO, 2009), 17–40.

4. Janice Holden, Jeffrey Long, and Jason MacLurg, "Characteristics of Western Near-Death Experiences," in Janice Holden, Bruce Greyson, Debbie James, editors, *The Handbook of Near-Death Experiences: Thirty Years of Investigation* (Santa Barbara, CA: Praeger/ABC-CLIO 2009), 133.

5. Alexander Strauch, *A Christian Leader's Guide to Leading With Love* (Littleton, CO, Lewis and Roth Publishers, 2006), 111–112.

6. Jeffrey Long, Paul Perry, *God and the Afterlife: The Groundbreaking New Evidence for God and Near-Death Experience* (New York, NY: HarperCollins, 2016), 73.

7. Jay E. Adams, *Christian Living in the Home* (Phillipsburg, NJ: Presbyterian and Reformed Publishing Company, 1972), 41.

8. C. S. Lewis, *Mere Christianity* (New York, NY: HarperCollins, 1980), 109.

9. The word *love* is used 552 times in 506 verses in the English Standard Version (ESV) Bible.

10. "Peter N NDE," www.nderf.org/Experiences/1peter_n_nde_6584.html.

11. "John R NDE," www.nderf.org/Experiences/1john_r_nde_6102.html.

12. "DW NDE," www.nderf.org/Experiences/1dw_nde.html.

13. "Camryn L NDE," www.nderf.org/Experiences/1camryn_l_nde.html.

14. "Harold R NDE," www.nderf.org/Experiences/1harold_r_nde.html.

15. "Erinn H NDE," www.nderf.org/Experiences/1erinn_h_nde.html.

16. "Trisha S NDE," www.nderf.org/Experiences/1trisha_s_nde.html.

17. "Lacy NDE," www.nderf.org/Experiences/1lacy_nde.html. Adapted.

18. "Natalie S NDE," www.nderf.org/Experiences/1natalie_s_nde.html.

19. Long and Perry, *God and the Afterlife*.

20. "Veronica W NDE," www.nderf.org/Experiences/1veronica_w_nde.html. Adapted.

21. "Carolyn B NDE," www.nderf.org/Experiences/1carolyn_b_nde.html. Adapted.

Discovering Divine Threads of Transforming Love

By Kathleen Kelly

*Thus says the L*ORD*, he who created you...who formed you...Do not fear...I have called you by name, you are mine.... You are precious in my sight, and honored, and I love you.*

Isaiah 43:1, 4 (NRSV)

I know this now. I did not always know that I was loved or even lovable. Nor did I have a clue how to love another. All of this had to be painstakingly learned.

Does everyone have to learn this, or are some people born *knowing* how loved they are and how to return the gift?

I first discovered this God who loved me and about whom I knew nothing through a one-sided battle of adolescent rage. I fell in love with this God, whose very isness is love, entered the convent at fifteen, left religious life at fifty-two, married a man twenty years my senior with six adult children, had a massive heart attack with accompanying near-death experiences, and through the whole of it learned that love's lessons never end. This is my story. Correction. This is God's story as told through my limited, flawed, and enticingly contradictory yet beautiful life.

Alternating Light and Dark

The fluorescent lights flashed furiously—light, dark, light, dark, light, dark—as nurses, doctors, orderlies (I know not who) clung to my narrow gurney, with me, barely conscious, bumping about upon it, racing through a long, dimly lit hall. *This is a nightmare,* I said to myself, *but I am going to wake up and I am going to be just fine.*

> *No one could hear the Voice but me. No words were spoken aloud. I felt the comfort of that Voice wrap me in its Presence.*

Oh no! a Voice corrected. *This is not a nightmare. It is very real, but you are going to wake up and you are going to be just fine.* I didn't know whose Voice it was or where it came from, but the last part of that sentence was spoken in stark contradiction to the urgency of the race to who knows where. The Voice was close, calm, even quiet as it reassured me: *It is very real, but you are going to wake up and you are going to be just fine.*

It felt like the voice of a caring parent tenderly encouraging a beloved child to go back to sleep. No one could hear the Voice but me. No words were spoken aloud. Where had I been just before the flashing lights and the bumpy ride rushing through the long hall? And where was I now? The atmosphere here was amazingly calm, quiet, semidark, and so very, very peaceful. A place absolutely without fear or hurry. I felt the comfort of that Voice wrap me in its Presence, and it was enough for me. There were no further questions here, only infinite tenderness and care.

How Had I Landed in the Hospital?

Had it only been earlier that same morning that my husband, Tom, and I awakened and set about decorating our home for Christmas? It was Tuesday, November 30, 2004. Tom's birthday would be in two days. My schedule for the next eight days was packed, so we decided to celebrate his birthday early with a nice dinner for family and a few friends, fifteen guests in all: Tom's children, grandchildren, my dad, and a few special friends. In hindsight, it probably wasn't a great plan, but I wanted the house to be fully decorated for Christmas by family arrival time at 6:00 p.m. We dove into the task at 4:00 a.m.

We unpacked seven or eight boxes of holiday décor, including our Christmas tree, eight strings of Christmas lights, Mr. and Mrs. Claus, multiple candles, and a large crèche with shepherds, camels, and kings, along with Mary, Joseph, and the Christ Child. The lighted evergreen boughs strung all along the point where the ceiling meets the wall throughout our great room nearly did us in. The Christmas tree was up, all aglow with colored lights. There was no time for ornaments, but I could live with that. Then with only a brief stop for a late lunch, we managed to sweep, dust, repack our now empty boxes with eleven months' worth of everyday décor, and stack them away just in time for me to begin making dinner.

We both hastily cleaned up and changed clothes, shifting into our more normal mode of operation. Tom left to pick up my dad. I quickly wrapped Tom's present, set the extra leaves in our massive dining table, and folded red satin napkins into a poinsettia shape, placing each one delicately in the center of our Christmas place settings, fifteen in all. I scrubbed the sweet potatoes, wrapped them in foil, popped them in the oven, prepared the broccoli for steaming, and seasoned the salmon. The decorated birthday cake and ice cream were all set for dessert. We were good to go. With every task tiredness claimed more and more of my body. *Thank goodness someone else is bringing the salad,* I thought.

As the family gathered so did the "oohs" and "ahhs" over the early Christmas displays in every room. While the gang bubbled with excitement as they chatted around the Christmas tree, I put the salmon in the oven and noted that dinner would be ready by 7:15. By now, nearly total exhaustion was embracing every bone and muscle of my body and seeping into my soul. *If I could just lie down for ten minutes, I would feel so much better,* I reasoned.

I slipped into our bedroom unnoticed. As I lay down, I couldn't get comfortable. I tossed every which way, to no avail. It felt like my chest was pinned inside an accordion and was being squeezed from side to side, front to back, top to bottom. Never had I felt so exhausted, with every muscle feeling inflamed and my left arm growing more numb by the minute.

Soon Tom came to find me. "Hey, are you okay? Do you have a migraine? Do you want some aspirin?"

"No, I don't have a migraine," I reassured him, "but you could bring me some aspirin anyway." He returned with the aspirin and water. Though I took them, I must have had an intuition that my heart was in trouble because I also muttered more to myself than to him, "I'm tempted to take one of Dad's nitroglycerin."

"I think I'll get Debby in here," he said. Debby, one of Tom's daughters, is a nurse. In seconds, she arrived, bringing along Tom's daughter-in-law, Barbara, who is also a nurse. I sat up, they looked me over, and asked some questions. Could it be dehydration? Sure, I certainly hadn't drunk much all day. Could it be low blood sugar? Yes, that has been an issue for me at times. So they brought me some orange juice, which helped me for a minute or two, but then the numbness was not only in my left arm but was also stretching across my back and into my right arm. They decided then and there that no matter the cause, I should go to the hospital and get checked out. Hopefully all I needed was hydration. I continued to fade as they led me from the bedroom to the door. My last words to my guests were haltingly spoken: "Take the salmon out at 7:15."

Several small miracles occurred that fateful night. Debby and her husband, Tommy, drove Tom and me to the hospital, which was only about five minutes away. Amazingly, there was not a soul waiting in the emergency room. How likely would that be on any night of the week? Tommy helped me into a wheelchair, because at this point, I could not walk. My legs were like rubber. As hospital personnel spoke with Debby, I broke out in a profuse, cold sweat and began to slide right out of the chair almost to the floor. Only Tommy's strong arms kept me awkwardly seated in the wheelchair. I think they took me to the back immediately and got me into a bed, but from this moment on I was in and out of consciousness. I did hear the ER doctor say I was in the middle of a full-blown heart attack.

Later I awoke in the heart catheterization lab just in time to hear the cardiologist say, "Now you will feel a warmth flow through you when I

> *Several small miracles occurred that fateful night.*

inject the dye." I did feel that warmth from my groin to the base of my heart, then I blacked out.

I fell again into that quiet semidarkness while that tender Presence, that comforting Voice, wrapped me in a blanket of sweet assurance and peace. I could have stayed there forever, utterly content.

Debby's View of That Night

When I went into the bedroom and saw Kathleen, she was very pale, reporting that her chest was feeling squeezed and her left arm was growing numb. These are all classic symptoms of a heart attack, but Kathleen is a woman who uses her treadmill, is usually full of energy, and both she and Dad eat healthfully; she isn't particularly overweight either. A heart attack just didn't compute for any of us in that room. It is amazing how denial can blind us to a reality we don't want to see. Thankfully, the reality of the situation quickly broke through our short-lived denial. We knew that whether it made sense or not, we needed to get this woman to the hospital!

The EKG strips were showing a massive heart attack happening right before our eyes.

When we got to the emergency room, no one was there, so they took Kathleen to the back while Dad and I filled out paperwork. Soon the emergency room doctor called for Dad and me to come back. We walked in and I saw the doctor standing there pulling EKG strips as fast as the machine spit them out. His eyes were huge. "What is going on here?" he asked in amazement.

The EKG strips were showing a massive heart attack happening right before our eyes. I don't think he had ever seen someone in full-blown heart attack before. Immediately, two nurses and I got Kathleen out of her jeans, into a gown, and prepped for a heart catherization. All of which seemed to take about two seconds. Kathleen was on her way to the heart cath lab before we could fully absorb what was happening. As I learned later, it was on that frantic ride that Kathleen heard a Voice telling her she was going to be all right. I wish all of us could have heard that Voice and felt that Presence.

An Upbringing Rooted in Family

I was born into a good Catholic family, the youngest of six. I am told that my mother almost died in childbirth. Her long recovery made it impossible for her to care for a newborn, so I was given to my godparents, my aunt Dolores and my uncle Myrl, to care for me through the first six months of life.

My bonding as a newborn turned into an attachment to my aunt and uncle, who adored me and spoiled me throughout my childhood. Having no children of their own, they kept their home organized, calm, and peaceful—a stark contrast to my home with three rambunctious boys, five, seven, and nine years older than me, and two sisters four and ten years older than me, who tried to keep the boys in line and make life peaceful— with small success. I loved spending several weeks every summer with my godparents. Upon returning home, my family, especially my brothers, were quick to inform me that I was "spoiled rotten." I learned to value being alone, trying to figure things out, often hiding from my brothers.

When I was nine, my family moved from our very small town in northern Ohio to the Turkeyfoot area of Akron, Ohio. There my parents found a Catholic church that felt completely different from the atmosphere of our small-town church, where the priest and sisters traumatized most of the families and students—or at least my family. Consequently, it was no surprise that when we vacationed at Turkeyfoot Lake and visited St. Francis Church, finding the priests to be welcoming, encouraging, and full of good humor, we moved to the lake community before summer's end.

My parents then took our religious observance to new heights. Being only nine years of age, I was considerably less enthusiastic about this new level of religious activity. The priest who befriended my parents was okay, but he was old. He had to be at least forty! In hindsight, I feel a little bit bad for the priests and sisters who did their best to get me and my siblings on board with my parents' newfound religion, but they had two strikes against them from our earlier experience. First, the trauma from our old pastor, who zealously preached fire and brimstone. And second, the sisters had been strict disciplinarians. One of them locked me in a pitch-black closet in first grade until I would tell her who did my arithmetic homework. I was a first grader! I had done my own arithmetic homework, but she wouldn't believe me, so back in the dark closet I went. The "God" these sisters and priest represented was pretty terrifying, and they all used the fear of punishment to make me be good. The priests and sisters at the new church were using all smiles and sweetness to make me be good, but I wasn't buying that act.

In my preadolescent brain, God was a grownup version of Santa Claus.

In my preadolescent brain, God was a grownup version of Santa Claus and the song we learned as kids: "You'd better watch out, you'd better not pout... He sees you when you're sleeping, he knows when you're awake. He knows if you've been bad or good so be good for good-ness' sake!" Santa Claus was always a larger-than-life figure in my family, so it wasn't all that far-fetched to meld God and the Claus figure into one. The "God" that all these adults talked about could hardly be *real*.

Externally I went along with the program, but my heart wasn't in it. By the time I was thirteen, my three oldest siblings were married and out of the house, and my brother, Ron, was away at boarding high school. My sister, Mary Lou, who is four years older than me, had progressively become (from my perspective) more holy-holy "goody two-shoes" and entered the convent at seventeen. That was a bummer on two counts. First, I inherited all the household chores that she did, which was abso-lutely not going to work for me, and second, my parents' friends along with my aunts and uncles started looking at me all smiley and asking, "So, when are you going into the convent?" Seeing my less-than-pleased reaction, they would chuckle or even laugh right out loud. I wasn't Mary Lou! I wasn't anything like her! Why would they ask me such a thing? More than once I ran to my bedroom and slammed the door, screaming "I'll enter the convent over my dead body!"

Leaving Home at Fourteen

After making it clear to anyone who questioned my future that the convent would get me "over my dead body," I found a way to escape from home. During the eighth grade I felt that it was time to get on with my life. *You can't be a kid forever,* I reasoned. *It's time to grow up.* I did not like the person I saw myself becoming: moody, secretive, boy-crazy, desperate to fit in—too desperate. It was time to make a move. With all of my brothers and sisters out on their own and my relationship with my mother growing increasingly testy, I decided to tell my parents that I wanted to go away to boarding school for high school. Ron was in boarding school and Mary Lou was in the convent for her senior year of high school. Why couldn't I go away to school?

I should have been hurt that my parents were all for it, but I wasn't. I was excited! I would be free to be me! No more peer pressure from various cliques at school, and my mother and I would have some distance while the household chores would be someone else's problem. The only stipulation was that I had to attend a Catholic boarding school. I chose a small all-girl's school in Pennsylvania just outside of Youngstown, Ohio. The school, named Villa Maria, was about a three-hour Greyhound bus ride from my home in Akron. The Villa was run by the Humility of Mary sisters, commonly known as Blue Nuns because of their sky-blue habits, which I liked, because they were bright and cheerful.

Sister Mary Dolores seemed to be everywhere I was, and I was pretty much everywhere I was not supposed to be.

The most memorable sister among the nuns was our principal, Sister Mary Dolores. She and I had a great deal of contact during my stay at the Villa, so I remember her face well. Her eyes were alarmingly steady, searching my soul for the least untruth. They were encircled by blue-black moons and years of wisdom and weariness. Her eyebrows were dark and thick. They knew all by themselves how to demand an answer, a *truthful* answer. One would arch itself high in her forehead and the other would dive low as though ducking a blow. She was a veritable black belt of the brows! In my freshman year, Sister Mary Dolores seemed to be everywhere I was. And I was pretty much everywhere I was not supposed to be.

You see, I thought that being away from everyone who knew me would be an opportunity to discover who I was, so I saw my first year at the Villa as a time of experimentation. Who would I be today? The class clown? The rebel? The hard worker? The actress, the instigator, the good student were all roles I would play in secret hopes that one of them would be a fit, one of them would be *me*. I would try these personalities on like dresses and discard them as easily as rejects in a changing room. I liked to see how these various approaches to the world would feel and what their effect on those around me would be. Poor Sister Mary Dolores. Her eyebrows were in constant battle sorting out my swiftly changing personalities.

Ninth grade, with all my trying on of various personas and avoiding anything religious, proved to be conflicting and difficult for me. Sister Mary Dolores threatened to expel me five different times that first year, but the fact that my goody-two-shoes sister had entered the convent and a very saintly priest had recommended me to the school saved me. Perhaps, too, Sister Mary Dolores saw something in me that I certainly could not see.

A Life-Changing Event

It was during the summer following my freshman year that everything changed, but not without a struggle between faith and despair. I had a boyfriend, Petey. We had been friends since fourth grade. I liked him. We hung out together quite a lot, especially during the summer, swimming and boating. He showed me my first garden of water lilies. And of course, he was cute, and I liked being with him.

One Saturday, Petey was to come to my house and help me mow the lawn, but he never showed up. When I called to find out what had happened, his older sister said he was really sick and they were probably going to the hospital. Three days later, Petey died of a brain aneurysm. I was shocked to my toes! Petey was just a kid like me. Kids don't die! He wasn't perfect, for sure; he got into his fair share of trouble, but he didn't deserve to die! Why would God do this to him?

No longer was the issue of God a matter of mere frustration. Now I was desperate to know if God really existed. I needed to know what life, and now death, was all about. No more trying on of personalities. Now I was on a mission.

I decided that when I went back to school for my sophomore year, I would join Sodality, which was comparable to a Bible or prayer study group. Of course, heads turned when I showed up, but soon the others ignored me. I asked nothing, I contributed nothing. I just listened, hoping to hear *something* that would help me to figure out who this "God" is, and if "God" really exists at all. About a month into it, the nun in charge was trying to teach us how to meditate. We were encouraged to spend about fifteen minutes in quiet and just talk to God. And though I listened, I never tried it. I'd have felt like a fool.

My Adolescent Encounter with God

One afternoon, however, I must have been in a pensive mood because I stopped in the chapel (which was more like a large church in size) and decided to give this prayer thing a try. It was about four o'clock, and I intended to stay for about fifteen minutes. The chapel was completely empty, and I sat in a hard wooden pew.

I remember looking up at the tabernacle and saying to myself, *Hello, little gold door, is anybody home?* I snickered to myself. *This is ridiculous. I'm talking to the wall, to air, to whatever!* But as I sat, I started to get angry, and soon I was screaming and raging at God—if there was a God. I let all my anger and fear come pouring out (inside, of course, not out loud). I yelled about my brothers and sisters leaving home; about Mary Lou being such a holy-holy, a Cinderella I was supposed to be like; about my mother and dad and how they probably hated me. Through tears I screamed about how unfair it was that God let Petey die. I accused God of terrorizing me with anger and fear. I was tired of being afraid. My tirade ended with this final blow: *"So, if You exist, I need to know it, 'cuz it will make a difference. If You don't exist, FINE! I got along without You before I met You; I can get along without You now!"*

I grew quiet then and rested there for what felt like another ten minutes or so. As I sat, I grew unusually calm. An utterly gentle peace descended upon me and blanketed me in its tender embrace. It was as though God was saying, *I understand. I am here, and I love you.* In those few moments, I fell completely, irrevocably in love with the

> *In those few moments, I fell completely, irrevocably in love with the One who was wrapping me in this healing presence.*

One who was wrapping me in this healing presence. I knew then that I was loved and I belonged, and that changed everything. I didn't want to move for fear that the presence I could almost taste would fade away, but even if it did, I *knew* that God existed and that would make all the difference.

As I left the church, I was amazed to see that it had grown dark outside. My friend Mary was running up the church stairs crying. "Mary, what's wrong?" I asked.

"There you are," she gasped. "Do you know they have the whole school looking for you? You missed dinner. You missed evening study hall. They are calling your parents and are about to call the police!"

It seems that I had been in the church not for fifteen or thirty minutes but for over four hours! While I couldn't account for the extended time,

A love affair with the Mystery that is God began that day and set the trajectory of my life in a new direction.

I knew I had not fallen asleep. As I look back on that day, which I have done many times, I know that while I sat in that pew I was taken to a safe place, a place where I was completely understood beyond my own understanding. A love affair with the Mystery that is God began that day in those moments and set the entire trajectory of my young life in a totally new direction. I am loved and I belong, and God indeed exists!

Back in the Hospital, the Family Gathers in Shock

The Christmas decorations, the lighted tree, the beautifully set table, the special meal now barely touched, the luscious birthday cake that would never be cut—all of these things that seemed so important just a couple of hours ago were now completely forgotten by both family and friends. Or worse, were a mockery to my prideful need to have everything "perfect."

While I was in the cath lab, Tom's daughter Debby was in the emergency room calling the family still gathered at our home and telling them that I was in the middle of a full-blown heart attack. A surgeon was on his way. This particular surgeon was widely acclaimed to be the best heart surgeon in town. He was also a member of our church, though we didn't know him personally.

When he met with the family, I am told that they hovered around him in a large semicircle while he attempted to bring them up to speed, but they all just stared at him as though he had eighteen heads. So he broke it down for them in words they understood but still could not comprehend. "She is deteriorating rapidly. We are going to salvage what we can, but even if she survives, she will never be the same." He paused then just long enough for the reality of the situation to sink in, and when it didn't seem to, he rephrased his message. "This is a salvage job. Quite frankly, she is dying." With that, Tom signed some papers and sat on the floor in a corner with a blanket over his head while the others just looked at one another in shock and the doctor headed to surgery.

Denise Tells Her Story of Waiting

My siblings tell me that as the on-call surgeon was speaking to our family, I was the only one to step up and ask questions. Truthfully, I have no idea what questions I asked, but I am pretty certain that each one was an attempt to stop our world from spinning out of control and to get this doctor to say *something* positive. *Anything* that would give us a sliver of hope. But no word of hope was forthcoming. He walked away, taking everything that mattered in that moment with him.

All hell broke loose with Dad, who flung his glasses aside and curled himself into a corner on the floor with a blanket over his head, apparently not wanting to see, hear, or accept any of this. The rest of us were too stunned to speak, left with this sick feeling inside, so utterly helpless. I felt the way I did that horrid morning when the World

Trade Center fell. I was standing on the promenade overlooking the Manhattan skyline and watched in disbelief as the second Tower and all that made the world feel stable came crumbling to the ground. Here I was again watching another kind of tower, my family, go helplessly into free fall.

Left with my own gut-wrenching thoughts, I, of course, started to think about Kathleen and what she had come to mean to us. I had been the most reticent of my siblings to fully accept her role in our family, but facing the possibility of losing her tonight, and the consequences of that loss for all of us, was a shocking wake-up call. Refusing to surrender to helplessness, I brought her face into my mind's eye and placed my hands on both sides of her jaw. In my imagination I *made* her look at me, clear-eyed and equally focused. I talked to her, demanding that she stay with us. Sometimes her eyes would glaze over and drift away. In a panic I'd draw her face back to me and tell her again that she *had* to stay. *No, no, no, don't look away! Stay focused on my eyes. Stay here,* I repeated endlessly.

Other family and friends started to arrive: Kathleen's sister, Shirley, and brother-in-law, Joe, who had just come into town to begin their six-month vacation in Florida; Sister Sallie, who had directed The House of Prayer with Kathleen, along with Beth, another friend who had known Kathleen for nearly twenty-five years. As word spread, more family and more friends found their way to the hospital floor where we Kellys had set up camp for the night. Whatever conversations took place, they were all done in whispers. The vigil remained eerily quiet.

My Journey with God into Love

Had I been in that waiting area and seen the pain and anguish on the faces of family and friends, I'd have been astonished. I had no idea that my little life was so valued by them. Oh, I knew that Tom loved me to the core, but the others? Really? It has always been difficult for me to accept that I am loved. I knew that God loved me. Oh yes! But that other people could genuinely love me? Well, I still had a lot to learn.

Ever since that moment in high school when I fell deeply in love with the One who *is* Love, I have trusted with every fiber of my being that God loves me, unconditionally and forever. That sophomore year I couldn't get enough of God. I read everything I could find. I spent hours sharing my God-findings with a friend, Judy, a junior who was as taken with knowing and loving God as I was. Somehow, I just *knew* that I was on a journey with God that would never be boring, that would be exciting, that would always show me something new and never end. Suddenly, I understood my goody-two-shoes sister. She had found God too. That's why she entered the convent.

> *Somehow, I just knew that I was on a journey with God that would never be boring.*

I desperately wanted to be good and holy, and the nuns seemed like the best place to start. When I told my sister about what had happened to me and that I wanted to enter the convent, she really tried to dampen my enthusiasm. "At least wait until you graduate from high school and then we can talk about entering the convent," she cautioned, even though she herself had not waited.

One evening on Easter break, while my mother and I were standing at the kitchen sink peeling carrots, I remember feeling like this was the right moment to break my pent-up news. "Mother, what would you say if I told you that I am thinking about entering the convent?" She stopped and looked at me quizzically.

"Are you?" she asked.

"Yes, I am," I declared, then quickly added, "I know it seems a little crazy and it doesn't sound like me, but God is doing something special here and I want to respond. I *need* to respond."

"But you'll wait until you graduate, won't you?" she said with a measure of alarm.

"I can't wait two more years," I said. The allure of God was overwhelming me *now*. I felt an urgency to respond now.

Dad kissed his crucifix and stood it on his dresser, as though to say, "I'm depending on You today."

Our conversation ended with Mother saying, "Let me talk with your father."

I sensed that Dad knew more about the ways of divine urgency than one might guess. After all, he was the one who took the lead in bringing our family "to new heights" in relationship to church and God. I also accidentally observed him one morning during his private prayer, kneeling by the side of his bed. I don't know how long he had been there, but as he rose, he kissed his crucifix and stood it again on his dresser, as though to say, "I'm depending on You today. Watch over us all." Dad is the one who went to Mass each morning even though everything was in Latin and he found it difficult to follow the English translation in his new St. Joseph Missal.

Dad was nothing less than honest and genuine at heart. He was a man of integrity with a great sense of humor to balance his earnest desire to be the best human being God knew he could be. It was no surprise that he gave me his blessing, no doubt curious as to what God was going to do with this contradictory daughter of his.

Moving toward Entering the Convent

I don't know what kind of conversation Dad and Mother had at the time, but I can tell you that throughout the spring and summer, they supported me but didn't push me or act as though the decision was a done deal. I sensed that I could change my mind at any moment, and they would be okay with that. The choice was mine. The only sticking point was that I wanted to enter the Carmelites, a cloistered community whose life was made up of manual work and prayer. My mother talked me into entering the same community my sister was in, with nuns who were either teachers or nurses. Her rationale was that visiting would be a lot easier on the family. They could see my sister and me in the same place and at the same time, rather than having to go in two different directions at two different times, or worse yet, having to go in two different directions at the same time.

That dilemma made sense to me, so I inquired with the Sisters of St. Joseph in Cleveland, Ohio. At the time, the sisters had a program where young women of high school age could finish high school while preparing to officially enter the community. The experience would be similar to boarding school life at the Villa, only we would live *with* the nuns. Ten other young girls and I made this choice in the fall of 1959. The sisters we lived with were young, happy, studious, a lot of fun, and very kind to us.

Junior year at the Sisters' Preparatory flew by, only interrupted by my brother Ron's wedding in April. I ended up being the maid of honor for my new sister-in-law, Kathy, because her best friend who was supposed to have that honor came down with chicken pox the week before the wedding. Since I was the only one who fit into her dress and shoes, I was elected to stand in for her. As maid of honor, I got to participate in all the festivities of the wedding party. At the reception, I tested my recent commitment to convent life by dancing away the night with all of my brother's college friends of the male variety. One of them asked "Why on earth do you want to enter the convent?" I don't recall what I told him, but he seemed satisfied and thoughtful with my answer. Later that summer, I fell pretty hard for the brother of a priest friend. In fact, we stayed in touch for several years. I didn't know until many years later that he had held off getting involved with anyone in hopes that I would leave the convent. That particular news made me sad, both for him and for me.

Growing into Religious Life

I loved everything I was learning in those introductory years. During my senior year in high school, which was officially my first year in religious life, I devoured the great spiritual classics, particularly the writings of Teresa of Ávila, John of the Cross, Reginald Garrigou-Lagrange, and Pierre Teilhard de Chardin. After graduating from high school, I received the long black religious habit of the Sisters of St. Joseph and began the first year of a two-year novitiate.

The first year was completely dedicated to manual labor, theological study, and prayer. The second year of the novitiate was the beginning of my life at St. John College, where I worked toward a bachelor's degree for the next four years. I loved taking theology classes at the college during the years of the Second Vatican Council when so many changes in the Catholic Church and religious life were taking place. These changes challenged Catholic sisters to go back to their roots and discover again why their religious communities were founded and claim again those initial experiences of faith that inspired their founders.

The Sisters of St. Joseph as well as many other religious communities discovered that their founders never intended the sisters to wear a habit that would make them stand out from the rest of the faithful. They were to be like "leaven in the bread," making a difference wherever they were by witnessing to the "great love of God" through their prayer and action. Consequently, in the mid-1960s, my community, as well as many other religious communities of sisters, exchanged their long black habits for simple modern dress, which was quite an adjustment for everyone concerned. I had worn that long black habit for about six years at that point, and I embraced the change enthusiastically. I felt like I was learning about my faith and its implications for my life all over again. It was an exciting time for me in our church and in my religious community.

I felt like I was learning about my faith and its implications for my life all over again.

Once I received my bachelor's in education, I immediately began my first year of teaching in a classroom of fifty-eight excitable, funny, and lovable first graders (yes, *fifty-eight* of them!). I relished their simple affection and trust, as I helped them phonetically sound out words and then reaped the reward of seeing their eyes light up with gleeful understanding as they would suddenly shout with joy, "I can read! I can read!"

All of my years teaching first graders were immensely rewarding for me. I was determined to do everything in my power to be sure that each and every one of those innocent and sensitive little ones would love school, love learning, and be completely assured that God loved them. On many weekends, I became part of adult teams who provided separate retreats for boys and girls, called Teens Encounter Christ. Those were wonderful years of not only growing in my own relationship with God, but also of being able to share some of that relationship with both youth and adults.

> *Those were wonderful years of growing in my own relationship with God and also sharing some of that relationship with both youth and adults.*

Further Education and Expanding Ministries

During the summers while I was teaching first grade, I was given the opportunity to earn a master's degree in literature and soon taught both English and theology at our Nazareth Academy high school for girls, eventually becoming one of its principals.

One of my last theology classes at Nazareth Academy was a group of sophomore girls vastly different in their social peer groupings. Some touted an attitude of being fast, flippant, and all too sure of themselves while others were shy, intimidated, and serious about school. A third group fell somewhere in between. I saw visions of my sophomore self in every single one of them. I couldn't help but smile, and in time, I shared my high school story with them. They listened in awe, and the walls between the groups started to come down. Trust grew among them and between them and me.

When Nazareth Academy merged with a coed Catholic school in the area, I chose to leave classroom teaching to go into pastoral ministry. Though I was offered several different positions, including Newman Ministry on a college campus, I chose team ministry at the Church of the Resurrection, a parish that built its mission upon a foundation of daily prayer as a team. We set aside one evening a week for prayer and contemplation. This was important for me because I had become quite the workaholic while teaching in a suburban high school along with living and ministering in a poor but blessed downtown Cleveland neighborhood. I needed a ministry that would help me to ground my work in an atmosphere of prayer and contemplation. It is all too easy to begin to believe that "my work is my prayer" and forget to take the time for the "one thing necessary" (Luke 10:42), deepening the bond of love with the One who is the reason for it all.

The Surgeon Returns: Sister Sallie's View

I awakened to a late-night call from Tom's son, Blane. "Sallie? It's Blane Kelly. This is difficult to say to you. Kathleen has suffered a massive heart attack tonight. She is in surgery right now. The doctor told us it is very, very serious." Silence. "It is very serious," he said again. I told him I was an hour away, but I would come right down. I got dressed and left immediately.

The ride was a long one. I kept talking to you in my mind, telling you I wasn't ready to let go of you yet and to please try to stay alive. I finally got to the hospital and found the Kelly family gathered. I asked where Tom was. He was crouched in a corner under a blanket. I'd hoped he was asleep. His daughters, Teri and Denise, were hovering over him. Denise was passing out blankets, trying to make sure everyone was comfortable.

A nurse came out and reported that the veins of your legs had been harvested and the bypass would now begin. Prayers flew from our hearts all over again. It seemed forever before she returned to say that the bypass was complete and the doctor would be closing you up. It was about 2:30 a.m. when the surgeon appeared. I watched his body language, trying to read it for any signal of what was to come. He looked exhausted and full of great concern.

He spoke directly to Tom, but we all gathered around to hear. He said the surgery had gone much better than he anticipated. You had survived it and were stable. The next twenty-four hours would be critical. He didn't offer any unwarranted hope about the condition you would be in when you woke up and he accepted no questions. You made it through the surgery and we held on to that. Thank You, God. I decided to go home and try to get a bit of sleep.

At 5:00 a.m., Denise called to say that you were bleeding internally and had been taken back into surgery. My heart sank, and prayers rose up again.

Lessons Learned at the Church of the Resurrection

I often say that I grew up at the Church of the Resurrection. Working with a pastoral team made up of two priests and two sisters was an exciting change from how most Catholic parishes are run. We were a *team*, and we shared dinner, evening prayer, and ministry. We celebrated Eucharist together with our community of parishioners each morning.

We team members took turns giving our personal reflection on the scriptures of the day. It was the first time that I would be in full-time ministry with adults.

I went through a three-year training course in pastoral counseling so that I could help my parishioners navigate temporary crises in their lives. Over time, this kind of counseling and hearing the pain people were experiencing became overwhelming for me, so much so that at times I could not eat. I literally could not swallow. With the help of a psychologist friend, I finally realized that many of those who were carrying the greatest pain were going through the death of a spouse or a nasty divorce, and that they would benefit from the care and support of one another as much or more than they could benefit from what

We all need to know that we are not alone in the tough times. Thus, peer-to-peer ministry was born.

I could offer them. We all need to know that we are not alone in the tough times. Thus, peer-to-peer ministry was born: widows and widowers, divorced and separated, and single-adult groups were formed, leaders were trained, and the ministry of these groups was truly blessed. Occasionally a parishioner would come to me for spiritual direction, a ministry that I found most helpful in my own life, so I received training as a spiritual director.

Through the Diocesan Retreat Center, I was invited to give occasional weekend retreats to adults on the subjects of prayer and our identity as God's beloved children. Ministry at the Church of the Resurrection was forming and shaping me. I was given multiple opportunities to teach, share, serve, and even build community through gathering both young people and adults to perform in a variety of plays and programs, such as our own versions of *Godspell* and *Up with People*. Most of all, life at Resurrection grounded me and supported me in my own spiritual journey as I celebrated with a loving community the presence of God within our mutual struggles and joys. I could only do my small part; God would have to do the rest.

Back in Surgery: God Doing God's Part

Barbara, Tom's daughter-in-law, was a nurse at the hospital where I received my quadruple bypass surgery. When she heard the code go over the PA system from the cardiac ICU, she knew something was very wrong. The surgeon had told the family that I was stable, but the code call indicated that all was not well. "This is bad," she whispered.

Soon, a surgical assistant came to see Tom. "Your wife is bleeding internally. We had her stable in the CICU (coronary intensive care unit), but now she's losing a lot of blood. We have to go back in and fix it. The surgeon has been recalled." With that, Tom signed more papers and found the floor again, unable to look at or speak to anyone.

"I felt like I was dying," Tom said later. "I didn't want to hear any comforting words because there weren't any comforting words to be said. Kathleen was dying and I wanted to die with her. I put a blanket over my head because I didn't want anyone to touch me or come near me. I was sure if they did, they would also be saying, 'I'm sorry, she's gone.' Those sickening words kept echoing in my head, and my gut clenched in revolt out of fear that those words would soon be true. I kept beating myself up for letting her work so hard to celebrate my birthday. I didn't need a birthday party—I needed Kathleen! If I wished for anything, I wished for this to be a nightmare, so I could wake up, and it would be over. If it wasn't, then nothing mattered anymore."

Two hours and forty-five minutes later I was again declared "stable" and was taken back to CICU. And for the second time my family heard the words, "The next twenty-four to forty-eight hours are critical." Only my awakening would reveal how much damage I had sustained. The reigning sense among the family was summed up in the hard words of my surgeon: "Even if she survives, she will never be the same."

Only family members could see me in CICU, and only one or two at a time. Every one of them report being shocked at how swollen and unrecognizable I was, with multiple tubes flowing seemingly in every direction while managing both the intake and outflow of oxygen, blood, miscellaneous drainage, and IV fluids. Everyone, that is, except Tom. His words to the family were, "Isn't she beautiful?" which only proves that true love is often blessedly blind. Or, as Antoine Saint-Exupery's Little Prince said, "It is only with the heart that one can see rightly." Clearly, Tom had begun to feel ever so little a sliver of hope.

Sister Sallie gained entrance to see me. Later she told me, "I took your hand and told you that I was here. You responded to my voice, fluttering your eyelids. I asked if you wanted me to sing, and you nodded yes, so I began to sing: 'Surely the presence of the Lord is in this place...' You can't imagine, Kath, how many, many people have called or emailed to ask about you and are praying for you. So many members of

> *The sense among the family was summed up in the words of the surgeon: "Even if she survives, she will never be the same."*

the Community of the Sisters of St. Joseph from Cleveland, the whole Rice School, Saint Cecilia community, and The House of Prayer folks. You are so loved and revered, Kath. Gosh, I am so glad to see you *alive*! I sang again, 'Surely the presence of the Lord is in this place.' I love you, Kath. You are never far from my thoughts or my prayer."

My Journey on a Pillar of Cloud

Was it while bleeding out in the CICU or during the second surgery that I became aware of being lifted up on a pillar of cloud? I am not sure exactly when it happened, but at some point, I became aware of being lifted up, up, up, slowly and steadily, on a pillar of cloud that continued to move toward a beautiful, almost blinding white light that was also surrounded by white clouds. I felt unbelievably light, as though my body was not on this journey upward. I became intrigued by this movement and the security of the pillar beneath me. I wasn't sitting. I was lying down, but there was no bed—just this pillar of cloud that felt very secure and yet incredibly soft. There was no pain, no fear, no concern at all, only weightlessness in a sea of peace.

The rising up seemed to pause while I gazed in fascination at the light. As blinding as it seemed, I could look at the light fully, without discomfort. I could feel myself surrendering completely to it. The light seemed to flow through me, as though I were translucent. It was an odd feeling that I had never experienced before. I was so completely transparent, so utterly *known* and *welcomed* exactly as I was. In the presence of this light, my foibles, insecurities, faults, and failures were of no concern at all—it was as though in this moment and in this place they weren't worth even remembering. I was so completely at home here.

After some time, I know not how long, I began to wonder where I was and what this pillar holding me was all about. Finally, I broke the peaceful silence and asked in amazement, *What is this?* Then I heard that Voice again. It was the same Voice I had heard earlier as I was being frantically wheeled down the hallway in the hospital. The Voice betrayed no gender, but in my heart, I knew it was the patient, caring Voice of the One who is Love. Almost as though it was waiting for my question, the Voice answered, "This is all the love and prayer that is being offered up for you." Those words fell upon me like pearl droplets, gifts of peace and promise. After a pause, giving me time to take in the

I heard that Voice again. In my heart, I knew it was the patient, caring Voice of the One who is Love.

sheer wealth of that message, the Voice continued. "You may use it to go on or to go back. The choice is yours."

Almost instantly I found myself responding, "Tom Kelly is *not* going to lose a second wife!" I could almost feel the Being behind the Voice smile as the clouds and the bright light slowly faded away and I was oh-so-gently grounded on earth, once again aware of my body, wrapped in a cloak of tender compassion and an unknown community of love and prayer.

Resting in that peaceful place, I began to wonder if it was rude of me to have answered so quickly, without fully considering the amazing choice I had been given, or even what the One behind that Voice might desire I would choose. Then I remembered that sense of a smile, a full and all-embracing smile that already knew what choice I would make. And it was good. My choice for Tom was affirmed, and I was utterly at peace.

The whole experience did not last long, though I was not aware of time or its passage, but its peace found a home in the core of my being and has never really left me.

Moving beyond the Sisters of St. Joseph

During the 1960s and '70s, even into the '80s and beyond, the Sisters of St. Joseph were struggling to understand their age-old and yet quite new identity in the Church and world after the Second Vatican Council. During those many years I threw myself into my ministries. As time passed, I began to feel less and less bonded with the Community of the Sisters of St. Joseph, even though my name was put forth multiple times for leadership in the community. Each time it was, I discerned that I did not belong in leadership. I loved my ministries, I thrived in my ministries, and I was grateful that the community gave me the freedom to engage in those ministries. But when I would endeavor to participate in the large gathering of sisters to determine our future, I felt more and more like I was on the outside looking in.

> *I loved my ministries, I thrived in my ministries, and I was grateful to engage in those ministries.*

At Christmastime in 1982 I flew to Florida to visit my parents, who had been living in Bradenton for many years. As my father and I were getting my luggage out of the trunk of his car, he asked me a strange question. "When you finish ministering at Church of the Resurrection where will you go next?" Without missing a beat, I answered, "Oh, I don't know. I'll probably go on sabbatical and write." *Where did that come from?* I wondered. I had never considered taking such a break from a ministry I loved, and though I had often wanted to write, I thought it was too unrealistic a venture.

From that moment on, though, I began to very seriously consider applying for a sabbatical in order to write. My father was also doing some very serious considering: how he and my mother might support this venture by offering the mobile home they rented out each season as my home for a sabbatical year. I applied to my community for a twelve-month sabbatical, and with my parents' offer of a home, a place to settle for the year, my request was so inexpensive that I could hardly be refused. The sabbatical was granted.

Going on Sabbatical

During my preparation for this venture, so many things fell smoothly into place that I had to believe God was indeed in charge. I inadvertently heard about a writer's workshop being led by a retired editor of a large publishing company. In brief, I attended that workshop and was able to spend the year writing as I had hoped. More importantly, though, my sabbatical became a whole new path of life for me in my relationship with God, my family, a new ministry, and a life-changing discernment about religious life.

At the start of my sabbatical year, I went on a thirty-day retreat at Bethany Spring, a small retreat center in Kentucky, near Gethsemani, the monastery where Thomas Merton lived, prayed, and wrote. I had made annual six- or eight-day retreats at Bethany Spring for several years before committing myself to a full thirty-day retreat.

When one chooses to spend thirty days in silence and prayer, broken up only by a one-hour daily meeting with a director, the movements of grace tend to be strong and frequent. God and I had many powerful encounters during those thirty days, each one challenging me to further stretch my capacity to love and to embrace a radical dependence upon divine providence, casting aside all fear of failure. Fear of failure had often immobilized me, and here I was going on sabbatical to write a book on a difficult subject that could cost me many relationships. How dearly I needed to depend upon God alone, come what may.

Halfway through my sabbatical year, my father had a heart attack and I temporarily became his caregiver and primary support of my mother and grandmother. His heart attack frightened me, making me realize how much we all—my grandmother, my mother, my siblings, and me—depended upon him in a thousand large and small ways. Fortunately, he recovered in a matter of weeks even without surgery. Seeing how vulnerable all three of them were, however, set me to thinking that one of us six children needed to be near them, and I was indeed the one who was most available.

> *Helping people who wanted to deepen their relationship with God was something I had been continuously growing toward.*

I began to consider what ministry I could do in Florida once my sabbatical and book writing were complete. Helping people who wanted to deepen their relationship with God was something I had been continuously growing toward, but the Catholic diocese where I was in Florida had no retreat center available where I could minister. It occurred to me that I might start one, a small one similar to Bethany Spring where I had made my thirty-day retreat.

Bethany Spring was founded and run by one sister, Sister Madelyn Abdelnour. Whatever made me think I could do this, I do not know, but I had been growing in radical dependence on God, so if God wanted this, God would bring all the pieces of the project together. And bring all the necessary pieces of the project together, God and a handful of others did. I became director of The House of Prayer in Fort Myers, Florida, supported by a seven-person board of directors.

The House of Prayer Ministry Grows

Within the first year, another Sister of St. Joseph, Sister Sallie, with whom I had ministered earlier at Church of the Resurrection, joined me in the mission of The House of Prayer. We gave many talks at different Catholic churches in the area and were welcomed in a host of other houses of worship, including Lutheran, Presbyterian, Methodist, United Church of Christ, Mennonite, and Episcopal congregations. In the areas of spirituality and ever-deepening intimacy with God, our doctrinal differences among the Christian churches played virtually no role. It is in our mutual desire for union with Christ, with the fullness of the Mystery of God, that we can find communion and common ground. The ministry of The House of Prayer multiplied, and the sense of community among those who participated became almost palpable.

As the ministry grew, so did our need for a larger house and more expansive grounds. That prayer was answered in great part through an Episcopal couple, whose prayer confirmed their need to move from their five-bedroom home on beautiful old Florida acreage in Alva to a more conveniently located home in town. Eventually, we were able to move to the house in Alva, where we were able to provide for more guests to experience weeklong private directed retreats, as well as days of prayer and many other faith-enriching programs.

Summertime in Florida at The House of Prayer was considered a very slow season, so my summers during those early years were spent at Creighton University in Omaha, Nebraska. There I worked toward and received a master's in Christian spirituality, all in an effort to make me a tad more competent for the depth of ministry we were undertaking at The House of Prayer. The study at Creighton served to ground me in Scripture and discernment, as well as to deepen my capacity to listen for God's movement in my directees through spiritual direction, as well as in my own life and prayer.

> *I received a master's in Christian spirituality in an effort to make me a tad more competent for the depth of ministry we were undertaking.*

First Meeting the Kellys

It was through The House of Prayer that I first met Tom and Betty Kelly and their daughter Teri. Teri had been a member of The House of Prayer board of directors when I first arrived in Fort Myers, and she encouraged her parents, Tom and Betty, to attend many of our Saturday Days of Recollection as well as other retreats and programs, which they happily did. I discovered that Betty had been diagnosed with cancer several years earlier, and she and Tom had been searching for ways to deepen their faith and their prayer. The House of Prayer seemed to be an answer to those needs.

Over the years, I came to know Betty and Tom and value them as friends. When her cancer became more aggressive and there was nothing more her doctors could do for her, Betty entered into hospice care at home. During the last few months of her life, I was privileged to become something of a hospice chaplain to her. While she was generally at peace, one of the hardest things for her to accept was not being able to do anything. Where in the past she was the one who gathered the family for both big and small celebrations, now it was up to her daughters and daughter-in-law to do all the planning, cooking, baking, and more while she merely sat and watched. That was painful for her.

One day as we entered together into a period of quiet prayer, she offered that pain to God and slowly came to realize that God still had something for her to do. God let her know that she had spent her life showing her family, as best she could, how to live and how to love. Now God was asking her to show them how to face and embrace death, trusting that life, from God's point of view, would go on. That experience with God gave her purpose, and as far as I know that is when she decided to write a letter to Tom and to each of her children.

In the last month before Betty died, I met with her and Tom to plan her funeral. She chose the readings and songs that had meant a lot to her. I merely wrote them down and prepared a funeral booklet, but the whole process felt very sacred to me, and I was humbled to be a part of it.

Getting to Know Tom Kelly

It was serendipitous that after Betty's death, Tom, while grieving, was also in need of a purpose, a peaceful place to grieve and still contribute. At the same time, The House of Prayer's board of directors purchased the Alva property that they had been renting, which would require that we do our own maintenance of the eleven acres surrounding it. The Kelly homestead was so similar to the acreage of The House of Prayer that I asked Tom to help us choose a riding lawnmower that would be up to the task before us. He did so. We purchased such a mower, and Tom taught me how to run it, which I did for a brief while. Soon, however, Tom found his way to The House of Prayer weekly to take over the mowing of the yard. Then he single-handedly built a pole barn to house the mower and other equipment so that the barn on the property could be repurposed into a meeting hall, complete with bathrooms.

> *I came to cherish Tom for his goodness, his simplicity, and his commitment to work hard.*

In the meantime, my mother and father had moved to Alva, which was a complete delight to me. Tom and my dad became great working buddies. I often thought of them as our St. Joseph, protectors and workers for The House of Prayer as St. Joseph protected and cared for the holy family. Over the next few years, I came to cherish Tom for his goodness, his simplicity, and his commitment to work hard and to do anything he could to help us out at The House of Prayer. Our regular participants came to value Tom and his quiet, faithful way of taking care of us all.

From Tom's point of view, he says that over those same years he had the opportunity to observe me from afar and loved how I interacted with people (even when he knew I was tired and needed a break). In his words: "I loved how you were a person who always took time for somebody else, no matter what you were doing; you stopped and paid attention to them, you took time with them and genuinely listened to them." He relished my joy in ministry and how I was aware of his need for an ice-cold cola in the middle of a hot Florida day, as well as his need to talk.

I guess over time we grew closer than either of us realized, but I was still shocked when one day he told me how he felt about me. Then quite spontaneously he blurted out something like, "I want you to marry me." I was dumbfounded and instantly aware of the absolute impossibility he was laying before me, yet I was also aware of how everything within me leaped in joy toward such an unattainable future. It made no sense. After all, I was a nun and he was a retired farmer twenty years older than me. It was completely illogical on so many levels. All I could promise him was that I would seriously discern what he was asking of me and give him my response. I think even *he* was shocked at the words that burst forth from him that day.

The Long Process of Discernment

Once again, I was caught in the throes of discernment. There had been other discernments and other men who over the years declared affection for me in a variety of ways and depths; each time I gently but firmly turned away their overtures, directing them toward God's activity in their care for me. I never gave any of those situations a full and gut-wrenching review. I was a vowed religious. What was there to discern? But I was haunted by the fact that apparently God was allowing this to come up again and again.

This time I was determined to enter into a complete soul-searching exploration of what I had assumed for over thirty years was my call and my vocation. This time I would not be the sole discerner. This time I would be brutally honest with a discernment group made up of a small group of sisters with whom I had lived and ministered, along with my spiritual director, a psychologist I began seeing weekly, and the leadership of the Sisters of St. Joseph.

This would not be a private discernment. It would be a communal one. And thus began a year-long excruciating exploration of what drew me to religious life in the beginning, how I had lived that life, why I made vows in the first place, who I made vows to. Was it the Church? The Sisters of St. Joseph? Or God?

Being an avid writer, I explored thirty years of journal writing to understand my thinking and prayer at different stages of my journey. I shared all of this quite openly with my community of discerners. I made three weeklong retreats over that year, *demanding* answers of God. I even resorted to ridiculous tests for God. And over and over again, the answer on every level—psychologically, spiritually, and communally— was clear, though I resisted it emotionally and spiritually.

Truth be told, at one point late in my discernment process I was so torn and so fearful of doing the wrong thing that I abruptly ended it. I told my discernment group that I was staying, that leaving the community was just not going to happen. I also told Tom. Though I valued his love and friendship, I would be staying in the Sisters of St. Joseph. My sister friends were relieved and pleased, though those who knew me best didn't really believe that the discernment was over, nor did my psychologist or my spiritual director—or Tom, for that matter. They just knew that I was overwhelmed with all the questions and the pressure I was putting on myself. No sooner did I make and let that decision be known than my gut knew it was the wrong decision, one I wouldn't be able to live with. I "tried it on" for a week or so but finally had to face what I had not wanted to face for so long.

Ironically, the sudden decision to stay became the final tumbler in the combination lock (which was holding me prisoner to indecision) that finally fell into place, opening the door to a potentially joyous and somewhat terrifying future. Was I actually being called to leave the religious life in which I had literally grown up?

I had resisted it vigorously until I was too exhausted to resist any longer. I knew I needed to risk leaving religious life, but I didn't want to be a "failure." I didn't want to be a disappointment to so many good people. I didn't want to cause scandal to all those with whom I had traveled on their spiritual journey. I didn't want to risk never being able to do this ministry again, and on and on. But God had been maddeningly clear with me in spite all of the confusing, contradictory, and frustratingly unclear aspects of the journey of my life: *If you want to go deeper in communion with Me, you are going to have to let go of everything, including your reputation, the security of your title, "Sister," the structures* of religious life upon which you have depended since you were fifteen years old. *There is so much more you have to learn that I cannot teach you in religious life.*

At fifty-two years of age, I took a deep breath, received a dispensation from my vows, and left the Sisters of St. Joseph.

And so, at fifty-two years of age, I took a deep breath, received a dispensation from my vows, and left the Sisters of St. Joseph, where I had learned so much, and where I had both fought with and benefited from their way of life. God and I were beginning a brand-new chapter.

So often when a priest leaves the priesthood or a sister leaves religious life, people tend to think that they are somehow "divorcing" God. Nothing could be further from the truth. These men and women have more than likely wrestled with God, their perceptions of God, their experiences of God whom they deeply loved, and found through it all that God is utterly faithful to their full becoming and is not inclined to accept anything less.

Beginning a New Chapter

I left the Sisters in the winter/spring of 1995 and allowed Tom to court me and I him. I knew all six of his children and learned a great deal more about them and the grandchildren. They told me numerous hilarious stories to help me get to know him and their family history better. He already knew my mother and dad, who thought he was pretty special, and I introduced him to my siblings and friends.

While many of my friends valued Tom very much, they were finding it hard to imagine that I would be happy with a farmer who was twenty years my senior. That picture just didn't fit with their image of me. They knew me as someone who wore heels and three-piece suits, had a couple of master's degrees, and gave talks and retreats all around the country. I assured them that if they really knew my interior landscape, they would know that Tom and I were a perfect match.

We married the following November. How did people respond to all of this happening? Well, Mother put it succinctly: "Oh, Kathleen, some people will be supportive and love you no matter what, and others will be all bothered, gossiping everywhere for a month or two, then everyone will go back to living their own lives." She nailed it. There were congratulations as well as whispers for a few months, but then when folks saw that we cared deeply for each other and that I was still invited to do God's work, our new reality became accepted and even celebrated. I have often

said that when I married Tom, I married goodness, I married contemplation (for he is a natural contemplative), and I married the earth.

Waking Up in the CICU

I have been told that the doctors and CICU personnel lost me several
times that night before I was finally stabilized and returned to CICU.
Once back in the CICU, I was put into a medically induced sleep, so
again, the wait for the family was painful and excruciatingly intense.
The family had been left with the strong implication that even if I survived, I would not be the same. Joy at my survival was seriously tempered with thoughts about who I would be and in what condition they
might find me upon awakening. Tom tells me now that all he could
think was: "I would give my life to see you smile again."

When Tom and his daughters, who had
never left the hospital, decided to go home
and shower, Tom's middle son, Blane,
tells me that he stood by my bed and held
my hand, full of wonder: *You're not out of
the woods. Will you be normal? I'm worried for
Dad. I'm worried for all of us. You worked your
way into our lives, and we worked ours into yours. Now you may not be around?*

*Joy at my survival was
seriously tempered with
thoughts about what
condition I would be in
upon awakening.*

Blane couldn't help remembering that his father-in-law, George,
also had heart issues on the same date, November 30, several years
before my heart attack. In his case, they put stents in and he recovered
the next day. Blane visited him in the hospital on December 1, and the
two of them watched a college football game in good spirits together.
"And George looked a lot better than you did," Blane told me recently.

Shockingly, on December 2, two days after his surgery, his father-in-law died of a massive heart attack right there in the hospital. All Blane could think of while standing beside my bed and holding my hand was that a lot of things could so easily go south. "You're not out of the woods yet," he whispered to my sleeping body. "Dad needs you; we need you. Please get well."

I wonder if I heard him. Blane tells me that as he was looking at me, I slowly opened my eyes and then looked toward him, struggling to focus on his face. I squeezed his hand and tried to say, "I love you." As I closed my eyes again, he hurried out to the Kelly camp still in the waiting area and announced the good news. Blane called the house: "She's awake! She squeezed my hand and mouthed I love you!" There were resounding screams and tears of joy.

"She's awake! She squeezed my hand and mouthed I love you!"

I slowly awakened in the CICU, unable to move or talk due to various tubes limiting both. Over the next five days, I was astonished at the family who came to see me. All of Tom's children arrived. Teri, Debby, Blane, and Denise were already in town before this event happened, but I was amazed to see Brian and Barry, and even Denise's boyfriend, Ben, who arrived from New York. How could this be, and why would they all come? It just would not compute.

I figured that I must have had a heart attack and bypass surgery. I remember hearing the ER doctor saying that I was in the middle of a full-blown heart attack. And I remember my mother being in the same condition after her valve replacement. But I could not understand everyone's presence and concern. Didn't they know I would wake up and be just fine, exactly as the Voice had told me? Even both priests came from our church and gave me the Sacrament of the Sick. In the days before the Second Vatican Council, it was called "last rites" because people were only given that sacrament if they were actively dying. Now it is called the Sacrament of the Sick and it must be well named, because with each day I grew stronger. I have such a clear memory, too, of Teri and Denise peeking around the door so as not to awaken me. They were such a beautiful sight, like two angels hovering near.

A Heavenly Visitor

After five days in CICU, I was moved to a private room, where Tom became anchored at my side. It was on one of the first days in my private room that I awakened to see a figure standing at the foot of my bed. As I focused on him, I could see that it was John, the husband of a dear friend—only John had died several years earlier. When he saw that I was clearly focused on him he said, "Remember what happened to me." And then he faded away.

John had had bypass surgery. He had been having some difficulty catching his breath after he and his wife would go on long bicycle rides or partake in other vigorous exercise. Although he had not been experiencing an immediate need, he and his doctor decided to go ahead with the bypass. The surgery went well. On the very day he was to be discharged, his vitals revealed a staph infection. A day or two later, he died.

I took John's warning very seriously and immediately called for my nurse. I told her about John, and I asked her to please put a sign on my door imploring every visitor to wash his or her hands or use sanitizer upon entering. When visitors came in, I apologized for the reminder, but I told them about John and how I did not go through all that I had already gone through just to get an infection and die. Everyone was very understanding. I am grateful to them for responding and to John for reminding me of how little a sacrifice it can take to keep another safe from untold pain, even death. I think of that every time I visit someone in the hospital.

Through the next three days, even more people came from church and various ministries in which I was involved. I continued to be mystified, though, by the visitors I received from the ER and CICU, folks who worked in those areas of the hospital and had ministered to me. Time and again they would say things like, "Wow! You sure had an angel on your shoulder!" and "You are a walking miracle!" I couldn't comprehend what they were talking about. By then I knew that I had had a heart attack and quadruple bypass, which was in itself shocking to *me*, but a lot of people have those. I wondered why I was a walking miracle. I had yet to understand all that I had been through and had put my family through.

> *I had yet to understand all that I had been through and had put my family through.*

I can't say enough about the care I received during my eight days in HealthPark Medical Center of Fort Myers, Florida. Every single person I encountered, from my wonderful surgeon and operating team to the floor nurses, practical nurses, and hospital cleaning staff, were all incredibly caring, competent, and kind. I experienced only one day of depression, feeling like my life would never be the same, that I would never have the energy I once had, that I would have to be hypervigilant about what I would eat, that my life was already somewhat used up. The literature I was given seemed to make it clear that the likelihood of another heart attack was a given. I felt like I would be walking on eggshells for the rest of my life.

Then *hope* entered my darkness when a woman about my age and build came into my room and introduced herself as someone who had had a heart attack similar to mine several years earlier. She was a volunteer at the hospital, and her job was to visit the cardiac patients and help calm their fears and answer any questions patients like me might have. We spoke for only half an hour or so, but my depression was gone. She was living proof that my fears were exaggerated and not based in reality. She was leading a full and happy life and still giving back. She strongly encouraged me to go to rehab, and most of all to hold on to trust. I took that to mean keep trusting that the God who brought me this far would continue to hold me close.

Leaving the Hospital

Going home held a number of adjustments. We laugh about how Tom gave Denise (our resident health advisor and vegetarian) permission to rid our cupboards, refrigerator, and freezer of any and all "junk food." Needless to say, what is junk food to a health-conscious vegetarian may not be junk food to everyone else. I didn't really care, since I didn't feel much like eating anyway.

Denise and Teri stayed with Tom and me for the next forty days and forty nights, taking care of our every need: cooking, cleaning, making sure that I took whatever medicine I was to take and that I took my short walks and kept my feet elevated while sitting. I worked with that little breathing tube and stubborn ball they gave me at the hospital until I was blue in the face, but after several days of trying, I still had to go back to the ER and have them clear the fluid from my lungs—not an entirely pleasant experience.

A month after my heart attack, our grandson was getting married and I wanted to go to the rehearsal dinner, wedding, and reception.

> *The long story of all that had happened finally came out. I was appropriately amazed and grateful.*

Teri and Denise helped me choose two new dresses, and Teri sewed at least a thousand red seed beads on my black floor-length gown that had outlines of red flowers strewn diagonally down the front of the gown to the floor. She said she wanted me to feel beautiful, and I did. Tom and I even danced at the reception, and not only slow dances, but a few swing dances as well! Several of Tom's children were terrified watching us dance like that, and I couldn't understand their concern. The home health nurse had removed all several hundred of my staples and had given me a good bill of health. Teri and Denise saw that I was eating better and walking every day up and down the long drive into our condo complex. I was getting stronger every day and doing well.

It was during one of our long afternoons of sitting with Denise, Teri, and Tom that I began to understand the concern I felt coming from all six of Tom's children. I was mentioning how surprised I was when personnel from the ER and CICU would come to my room and say things like, "Wow! You are a walking miracle!" or "You sure had an angel on your shoulder." What was the miracle? I didn't get it. They just looked at one another as though to say, Should we tell her?

Apparently, they decided that I was strong enough to hear how dire my situation really was, and how they were told that even if I survived,

I would never be the same. The long story of all that had happened finally came out. I was appropriately amazed and grateful. I also gained a new respect for my very scarred body with its telltale signs of where hundreds of staples up and down both legs and chest had been. If this body survived everything they had just told me, I had better take good care of it. My body deserved that. God and all those people who prayed for me deserved that.

When I was allowed to begin rehab, I gave myself to it 100 percent. I wanted to know how much I could do before the rehab therapists would tell me to slow down. After twelve sessions I thought I was finished and was pretty excited that I had achieved nearly all the markers my cardiologist had set out for me. Imagine my surprise when my therapist told me that I was not signed up for twelve sessions, but twelve weeks of three sessions a week! I finished those sessions and am so very glad that I did, because they not only gave me a good sense of how much work my heart could handle, but they also helped form a habit of challenging exercise that I maintain to this day, fifteen years later.

Looking Back over Our Twenty-Five Years of Marriage

Tom and I celebrated our twenty-fifth anniversary in 2020, and so it became an occasion to look back on our journey with all of its ups and downs (which has a way of becoming "ups," as the gift of hindsight often offers us). As one might imagine, I experienced some adjustment during our first years of marriage while trying to fit into the large Kelly family. They knew very little about me, other than I had been a nun, so I think I got put in a box of sorts. Tom's brothers and sisters as well as his children had all experienced nuns in one way or another, so the thought that he would be marrying one of them was just kind of weird.

It was something of a challenge to navigate becoming part of the closely knit network of Tom's six children, who were full of both good-hearted humor and genuine concern for their dad. They were all adults who lived in various parts of the country, but they were in constant communication about all that was happening in their dad's life, and they were clearly protective of him and of their mother's place in all of their lives. Honestly, I could not, and never wanted to, take their mother's place in the family. I did not feel threatened by their love for Betty. In my own way, I had loved her, too, and I made it clear to them one Christmas.

I had found an especially beautiful photo of Betty. I had it enlarged and framed. I wrapped up a copy for each of them, including Tom. When we were all together on Christmas Eve, I gave it to them. I explained that their mother was and always will be their dad's first love. She will always have that place in his heart and in their hearts. I value that and would never want that to change. I told them that I am grateful to Betty, because Tom and each one of them are who they are today, in great part, because of her and her love for them. The gift I gave them is meant to be a lasting celebration of her in all our lives. I was in tears, of course, and so were several of them, but all were warmly responsive.

My Mother's Death and an Important Revelation

Two years after we were married, my mother's congestive heart failure was becoming more aggressive. She had had aortic valve replacement a decade earlier, and scar tissue was forming, closing off the new valve. Tom and I stayed with my parents during her last weeks. It became a holy time with my mother, revisiting many family memories, both the beautiful ones and the difficult ones.

As we recalled all the birthdays we had celebrated together (since her birthday was the day before mine), I had the perfect opportunity to ask her how it was for her to have spent her whole birthday so many years ago in the hospital trying to give birth to me, who was apparently quite stubborn about coming out. She just smiled and said, "Oh, that was nothing." Then she grew quite serious and added, "The real pain was not being able to leave the hospital with you. You can't imagine how horrible it was not to be able to take care of you for so many months. Not to experience your first smiles and giggles, and all of your changes in those early months. I was missing out on so much." She wept; we both wept.

I am ashamed to say it, but that was the first time I was able to see our separation at birth from my mother's point of view. All the years until that very moment, I had always felt that somehow, in some deep place inside, I wasn't really wanted by my mother. *Why should she want me?* my unconscious self had said. *My very birth nearly killed her!* Of course, I had also always known that that feeling was crazy, illogical, and I had ample experiences of her self-sacrifice and love to prove my feeling wrong. But feelings have a way of just getting buried under the burden of logic.

With the aid of God, Tom, and my mother, I was able to fully embrace not only divine love, but also human love without reservation.

God and I had worked long and hard over the years to be freed of the lie of not being wanted that I had stifled with logic, but that day something was absolutely set free in a very deep place inside of me. I believe that it was the capacity to accept being loved, just for who I am, not linked in any way to my accomplishments. It was then, with the aid of God, Tom, and my mother, that I was able to fully embrace not only divine love, but also human love without reservation, and I can't thank my mother enough for that precious moment between us. I am not sure I would have ever been able to fully, unconditionally, accept Tom's love or give myself fully, unconditionally, in return without it.

Another day, my mother asked me how it would be when she died. What would it be like to die, and what would she find waiting for her? At the time, of course, I didn't know how to answer her questions, so I told her what the doctor told us: when her aortic valve finally closed completely, it would feel like someone turned off the lights. Then we talked about what our faith had to offer us. That a different kind of life awaits us, and *that life* will be wonderful beyond anything we can imagine in this world. We prayed together, shared the scriptures, sang together, and just talked the day away. She seemed comforted by our conversations and our songs. My parents' sixty-fifth wedding anniversary was on June 8, 1997, and my mother peacefully left us for her new life on the following day.

I realized that my mother had taught me how to love and how to die.

The hospice nurse and I bathed her body; then my father and I blessed her eyes, her lips, her heart, her hands, and her feet, thanking God in turn for the goodness we had experienced through each part of her precious body. Tom and my friend Sister Sallie joined us, and as we processed to the hearse we sang, "May the angels welcome you to paradise, and the martyrs greet you on your way. May you see the face of the

Lord this day. Alleluia, alleluia." I realized that, just as Betty had taught her children how to love and how to die, my mother had done the same for me. My father and I became even closer as he heroically dealt with his grief over the next few years by volunteering to help others in his community and in his church.

Weathering the Storm of Threatened Bankruptcy

During those years after my mother's death, an agreement was made between the Tom Kelly family and the Ed Kelly family (Tom and Ed were twins) to develop the eighty acres, including an eleven-acre lake, on which several members of the two families lived, including Tom and me. Tom and Ed had always seen the eighty acres as their children's inheritance, with lakefront acreage deeded to each of them. Trying to develop that property was a huge venture that nearly drove Tom and me into bankruptcy. Tom and I borrowed heavily against our property, and because we actually lived on it, we were especially vulnerable.

The threatened bankruptcy seriously challenged my sense of security, something that had never been threatened in the Sisters of St. Joseph. God was definitely dealing with me in a way that showed me firsthand what so many people deal with on a daily basis. We prayed to know what to do, and we prayed for the capacity to be totally dependent on God, while at the same time taking responsibility to do all we could to keep us from losing everything. We agonized over every decision. When I felt myself shaking as though overwhelmed with impending doom, my heart trembling like a frightened bird, God would enclose my heart in loving hands, clothing me in Presence.

Thankfully, the venture ended well when we sold the acreage to another developer, but it was touch-and-go and absolutely terrifying for those of us who were most at risk. I don't know how many times during those few difficult years Tom and I had to remind ourselves that we had each other, we had a roof over our heads, and we had our faith. And if we lost even the roof, we had our faith and each other. I remember Tom's daughter Debby telling me during an especially scary time that if we had to declare bankruptcy, she would deed her lot back to us. Though we hoped it would never come to that, I found her offer to be loving and wonderfully comforting.

God Partners with Tom and Me in Ministry

When we were able to sell the homestead, Tom and I moved into a nearby condo. I continued giving talks and offering spiritual direction in our Catholic communities, as well as Episcopal and Presbyterian communities throughout the west coast of Florida. I also gave retreats in North Dakota as well as with the Mennonite community in Pennsylvania. Sister Sallie and I continued to train spiritual directors for the diocese of Venice, Florida. I directed retreats for the diocesan School for Pastoral Ministry and the diocesan retreat center that had been recently built in Venice.

Ministry was very much alive in my new life as Tom's wife, and while it added to my stress level, it also brought me joy.

Ministry was very much alive in my new life as Tom's wife, and while it added to my stress level, it also brought me much joy. As much as possible, Tom joined me in each of these opportunities. He was especially beloved by the Mennonites. I think they saw in him the simplicity of life that was core to their way of being. Tom gave none of the talks or teachings. He merely attended what he could and joined in conversation at meals and on breaks, yet individuals sought him out for what words of wisdom he might offer. They valued him, trusted him with their concerns, and missed him terribly if he didn't accompany me. And this reaction from those who experience him remains true to this day. I still tell people that when I married Tom, I married goodness, I married contemplation, and I married the earth.

Dad Suffers a Stroke and Life Changes Again

It was on a day that I was training spiritual directors in Punta Gorda, Florida, that I got a call from Tom. My father had suffered a stroke. He and I had had lunch together just the day before. How could this be? I immediately drove to the hospital in Fort Myers where he had been taken. His stroke affected his left side and his speech, so at ninety years of age, my strong father, who could build and fix just about anything, had the long road to recovery ahead of him.

When he was released from rehab after regaining his speech and basic functions, he moved in with us. He was ready to push himself because he wanted so badly to be able to play tennis again. Tom and I took him to wheelchair tennis, and his lights came on, so to speak. He could use his right arm and right leg, so with racquet in hand, he would use his right foot to push and pull his wheelchair every which way to get to the balls I would hit to him.

When he realized that he could play again, I told him he had to stand up. Tom would stand behind him holding on to his belt, while

I hit balls close to him, forcing him to step to one side or the other to reach the balls I hit. Eventually, he was again able to play tennis unassisted. His determination and drive became truly inspiring to me and to all who knew him. Was he 100 percent? No, but he was living again.

Dad lived with us for a year or so until he wanted to live on his own, which he did for several more years while Tom and I "took care" of him from a few miles away. As time wore on, Dad would often get his days and nights mixed up, so he would call us at about three in the morning and in a chipper voice ask, "So, what are we going to do today?" While it was both humorous and frustrating caring for his many yet simple needs along with his adamant assurance that he could still drive, I would give anything to have him call me at any hour right now and ask in his chipper voice, "What are we going to do today?"

It was at some point during those few years of our caring for Dad that I had my heart attack, and for several months I was unable to care for him at all. At the same time, he was beginning to need even greater help, so my brother and sisters, who all lived out of state, came to visit and convinced Dad that he needed to move into an assisted living community where he could—and did—thrive until his death at ninety-seven.

As I look back, I can clearly see that my parents and their sixty-five years of loving marriage taught me a great deal about living life to the fullest no matter the circumstances. I witnessed them both enjoying abundance when it was given and surrendering to its absence when necessary, and they did so with grace, dignity, humility, great faith, and good humor. My siblings and I can only aspire to the profound lessons Mother and Dad taught us without their even realizing it.

Finding New Beginnings in Tennessee

Four years after Dad's death, Tom and I decided to move to the mountains of Tennessee where we had vacationed many times in previous years. We had purchased a little mobile home there on a lovely lake, and so we sold our Florida home and became what Tennesseans call "Yankee Move-Backs." We have become part of a wonderful church community very much like the one we called our home in Florida. I have done some hospice chaplaincy in this town, some outreach in the community, and I continue to teach and participate in a few ministries at our church.

I am so grateful to be able to continue to serve and to share what God has so freely given to me, even though I know that I am entering into those years of "surrender" that I observed my parents so gracefully embrace. Tom is ninety-eight now, and my greatest joy is sharing life with him. He has promised me ten more years, so I have my marching orders. I need to remain as healthy as possible physically, emotionally, and spiritually so that I can keep up with him and all that life offers us. We feel so blessed that two of Tom's children, as well as a grandson, his wife,

> *I find myself grateful for my heart attack, for I believe that the fear, love, and concern surrounding it catapulted me into the center of the heart of this family.*

and five great-grandchildren, have moved nearby; we stay in close touch with my brother and sisters, and their children and grandchildren, as well as Tom's children and their families who live long distances away. There is nothing like the blessings of family and the fun of all the texting and emailing we do on a daily basis.

I find myself grateful, too, for my heart attack itself, for I do believe that the fear, love, and concern surrounding it managed to catapult me into the very center of the heart of this beautiful family. It changed me—it changed all of us—and I couldn't be more humbled or feel more blessed.

"Every vocation," writes Thomas Merton, "is a mystery, and no juggling of words make it any clearer. It must remain a contradiction" (*journal entry, Vol. 3, November 15, 1957, 137*). I surely do see the two halves of my life as a contradiction to each other, from one point of view. From another point of view, I see how each is a fulfillment of the other.

Perhaps all of us have questions about our life's journey, about "the road not taken," or about what God really desires of us, and whether we have been a disappointment, or a joy, or both to the One who made us. Fortunately, God knows the mystery that each of us is, and I do absolutely believe that the important thing to know and embrace is that: God *is*, we are loved, and we belong. As the medieval mystic Julian of Norwich reminds us:

> All shall be well, and all shall be well, and all manner of thing shall be well
> ...for there is a Force of Love moving through the universe
> that holds us fast and will never let us go.

This is my story, and it is God's story, told through my life, yes. But it is also God's story told through each of our journeys, if we can just find and follow the thread of transforming love God has been weaving through our decades of ups and downs, twists and turns, and seemingly contradictory yet remarkably beautiful lives.

My Life since My Near-Death Experience

Kathleen Kelly

Since that experience fifteen years ago, I am more acutely aware of God's presence in my own life and in the lives of all of us whether we realize it or not. I am willing to share my experience when it seems right, but I feel certain that the issue isn't all about me—it is about all of us.

I believe that God is passionate about every single one of us and only desires entrance into our hearts, minds, and lives; that alone will make all the difference. If my story helps to open those doors, great. If it does not, then I trust that God has countless other ways and means of knitting those precious threads of transforming love into our lives, even if we remain unconscious of them for many, many years.

Q *How has your NDE impacted the decisions you make in your life?*

A My instantaneous reaction to having been given a choice to go on or go back was "Tom Kelly is not going to lose a second wife!" That choice has guided my decisions as to how I will spend my time and the priority I give to those choices.

At the time of the NDE I didn't say, "O Lord, I have to go back. My directees need me. I have talks to give, retreats to plan." No, everything in me knew even then that my life with Tom Kelly must be my priority. Of course, I have enjoyed and still enjoy a variety of ministries, but they are not my first priority. My marriage to Tom, along with God's place in our marriage and the life we share, will always come before any other commitment. That awareness has just deepened and strengthened over time.

The fact that God gave me a choice continues to astonish me. I don't know why God did that, or if that choice is offered to everyone in one form or another, but it amazes and humbles me that God should lay so significant a choice before me. It says something about the mutuality of our relationship. God seeks my input. God cares about what I think and how I feel. My desires matter to God. That is rather shocking to consider. It is not that I didn't already know this on some level, but this NDE was a kind of proof of it. And so I trust the mutuality of our relationship even more emphatically.

Q *What did your NDE teach you about love's lessons?*

A When I was told that the pillar of cloud was "all the love and prayer being offered up for you," I was a bit overwhelmed, since I was not aware of being so valued. Since that time, I have taken that message to heart and it has very seriously influenced my prayer for others. No one needs to feel alone in the tough times. Others need our love and our prayer, and though I don't know *exactly* how it all *works,* I do know that our love and prayer can hold another up, hopefully long enough for that person or persons to see the light and experience hope, peace, assurance, love, tenderness, and all that God desires to offer.

Q *How has God's love transformed your life?*

A When I look back at the entire NDE experience as a whole, I am overwhelmed by the continued presence and detailed elements of care and protection God was offering me: the first encounter with the Voice reassuring me that this was not a nightmare and that I was going to wake up and be just fine. Then the complete sense of assurance and peace when I blacked out during the heart cath. The pillar of cloud with its clear choice of going forward or going back that God lay before me, followed by John's visit reminding me to be clear-eyed and careful about avoiding preventable infection. Why should God do all of that for me? I "deserved" *none* of it, yet I was given *all* of it.

As if *that* were not enough, I was given unbelievable care by everyone at the hospital, the woman who eased my fears and depression, by every member of my family (even our grandchildren and their wrestling teams, who sent flowers and welcomed me back to their meets) and especially those blessed forty days with Denise and Teri. I received stacks of cards and calls from friends in every group of which I was a part. Vigilant rehab therapists, one of whom stayed in touch with me for several years. My surgeon, whom I met up with again at a church dinner dance about six months after surgery. I was able not only to thank him but also to demonstrate what a great job he did by dancing several swing dances with Tom that night.

God has been looking out for me my whole life, and I venture to say that God has been looking out for each of us, without our realizing it. I was just fortunate to have had a life-threatening experience that made me so completely vulnerable and utterly unable to do anything for myself that I was finally in a position to receive all that God chose to give me, and I couldn't be more grateful.

I continue to be encouraged and assured that a marvelous experience of tenderness, compassion, unconditional love, total welcoming, and acceptance awaits me. I believe that experience awaits each of us. I am rather excited to go there, though I know I must still have work to do since I haven't been called there yet. I do not fear death. I see it as a doorway to the greatest love story into which one could ever hope to be drawn.

No Fear in Heaven

By Kathy Shields, as told to Jeanette Levellie

We love because he first loved us.

1 John 4:19 (NIV)

It was the middle of April 2018, just a few months after I got home from the hospital. I was watching a movie with my daughter, Kelsha. After the movie was over, I turned to Kelsha and asked, "Did I talk about my mom when I was in the hospital?" She just stared at me—and that's when we started talking about what had happened to me three months earlier.

The Blackest Night

On the evening of January 7, 2018, I sat at the kitchen table with my twenty-year-old twins, Kelsha and Kacey. The three of us chatted as we shared a bag of our favorite barbecue chips. "I can't stay up too long," I said. "I need to get to bed early." I hadn't been feeling well, so I was going to see my doctor first thing the next day. I glanced at the clock, which read 9:00.

"How was work today, Kelsha?" I said. "Do you enjoy selling office supplies and filing?"

"Yes, all but the phone calling to try and drum up more business. I get so nervous." Kacey nodded in sympathy and patted Kelsha on the shoulder. Being the quieter of the two, he could relate to her shyness about talking to strangers.

I smiled. "You'll get used to it. A year from now, you'll be a pro." I reached for another chip. As I put it in my mouth, I also took a deep breath. The room started to spin. Kelsha and Kacey's faces blurred. I gasped to catch my breath. And then, blackness.

Kelsha's Story: The Worst Day of My Life

Sunday, January 7, 2018, was unusually cold and icy, even for winter in Paris, Illinois. I had returned home a few minutes before from visiting a friend, slung my heavy parka onto the back of a kitchen chair, and sat down to visit with Mom.

My mother is the best friend I've ever had. She's been a source of help and encouragement 24/7 for my twin, Kacey, and me. Both of us have health issues that require constant care. But in twenty years, I've never heard Mom complain. Her faith in God has remained steady, and she's encouraged us to be and do our best in every endeavor. She was, and still is, our rock.

Mom smiled as she reached for another chip. Without warning, she started to slump over in her chair. I raced around the table.

"Mom! Mom! Are you okay?" Her body slumped onto the table, face down. I knelt beside her chair and gently pulled her onto the floor beside me. Three times, she exhaled and then gulped for air in huge gasps. Then she went completely limp, falling sideways onto my right arm. Her body was still.

Terror filled my brain. My heart pounded in my temples. I began to sweat. "Mom, Mom!" I screamed over and over, trying to get her to respond. I felt so helpless.

"Kacey, call 911," I screamed to my brother, who was standing nearby, frozen, his eyes filled with worry.

I'd never had to take over in any kind of emergency, and I'd only seen CPR performed in TV shows. *What to do, what to do?* I cradled Mom's head in the crook of my elbow, as if she were a baby. Time stood still. When Kacey connected to 911, he handed me the phone. I screamed into it, "You have to help me! My mom has passed out and is slumped over. I don't know what to do!"

> *I cradled Mom's head in the crook of my elbow. Time stood still. I screamed, "You have to help me!"*

The 911 operator asked for our address. She told me to try and clear Mom's mouth of any food or other obstructions. I did my best, but my hands were shaking uncontrollably. I kept shouting, "Someone, help me! I need help! This is my mom!"

Questions fired at me from the phone. "Is she breathing? Can she respond? Is she moving?" All I could manage was "I don't know! Hurry, please!"

To Mom I said, "You may *not* die on me, Mom. Kacey and I need you. Dad needs you." *This can't be happening.*

"Try to calm down," the operator said. "An ambulance is on the way." Over the phone, she calmly instructed me how to compress Mom's chest to try to get her to breathe again. I made a meager attempt to push down with force. Since I'm just over five feet tall and slender, my best efforts weren't very forceful. I made twenty or so compressions while the operator stayed on the line, firing question after question at me. *God, please help me!*

After what seemed like thirty minutes—but was probably only five—we heard a knock on the door. *Why on earth are you knocking?* I thought. *My mom is unconscious and not breathing, and you knock on our door?*

"Come in," I shouted. Kacey ran to open the front door and let the EMTs in, and he showed them to the kitchen. Mom's lips had taken on a blue tinge. "She's here," I screamed to the EMTs, who seemed to be moving in slow motion. "Hurry, hurry," I kept hollering. I laid Mom's head gently onto the floor, then started moving everything—the trash container, a step stool, the ironing board—out of the way so they could bring in the gurney. I was sobbing the entire time.

They finally got the gurney into the room and knelt down beside Mom to feel her pulse. "Is she dead?" I asked.

The EMT with black hair and dark eyes stared at me, silent. Finally, he spoke. "We won't know until we get her into the ambulance."

In the background, I heard Kacey calling Dad, who worked the night shift. He spoke very slowly and methodically. "Dad, this is Kacey. You need to come home—something's happened to Mom." *How can he be so calm?*

I jumped up and grabbed the phone from Kacey's hand. "Dad, Mom collapsed!" I shouted into the phone. "Please, get here now! The EMTs are here, but we need you."

The EMTs got Mom's limp body onto the gurney and then wheeled her outside, down the driveway, and into the ambulance. I rushed outside after them, through the icy, muddy front yard, and stood beside the ambulance, peering through the window. When one of them got out the paddles to shock Mom's heart, I turned away and ran into the house. I couldn't watch.

Inside the living room, I collapsed onto the floor. Prayers gushed out of my mouth before my knees even hit the carpet. "O God, please forgive me for all the stupid and messed-up things I've done. Please don't let me lose my mom. Forgive her, too, if she's done anything that wasn't right." Fear washed over me. I was drowning in a sea of desperation. "Please keep her alive, Lord. We can't lose her."

> *I felt like I was fighting a huge giant named Death, and God was the only one who could help me overcome it.*

Before today, I'd never prayed aloud. I'd been a Christian since I was sixteen and I talked to God a lot, in my heart, silently. But now, with my face on the floor and my heart along with it, words tumbled out in spontaneous gasps. I felt like I was fighting a huge giant named Death, and God was the only one who could help me overcome it. If someone had to die, I wanted Him to take me instead of Mom.

Tom's Story: A Horrible Nightmare

I was working the night shift when I received a phone call from our son, Kacey. I work in the back toolroom of a plant that makes headlights for cars. I'm pretty much alone, but I always have my cell with me in my toolbox, in case someone needs to reach me. The machine I was working on was loud, so I didn't hear my phone ring until Kacey called the third time. I could tell he was having a hard time getting the words out and I couldn't understand him. "Calm down, Kacey. Take your time."

"Dad! Come home now," he said. "Mom can't breathe. We don't know what's wrong with her!"

I asked him if anyone was there with him. "Yes, Kelsha is here, trying to get Mom to breathe, and an ambulance is on the way." Then I heard Kelsha's voice sobbing and shouting after she yanked the phone out of Kacey's hand.

"I'm on my way, honey." I shoved the phone in my back pocket and shut down the machine I was working on, and then I raced through the plant as fast as I could make my legs work. That three or four minutes seemed like a year. "God, please be with my wife and kids. Please don't let this be happening. Help us, Lord."

> *I knew Kathy was God's choice for a mate, and I couldn't fathom doing life without her.*

I didn't even look at my speedometer on the five-minute trip home. All I could think about was getting there. My heart was hammering. Even though it was the coldest winter we'd had in eight years, I could feel sweat trickling down my face. To think I might be losing Kathy, my soul mate, terrified me.

Before I met Kathy, I'd had several unhealthy relationships. So I had begun praying that God would send me the right person who would love me and be faithful to me. I also made a promise to God that I'd be faithful to whomever He sent me.

Kathy and I met in 1986 at a party and became friends. Both of us were comfortable with each other, and we could talk about anything. We dated for two years and really got to know each other. We were married in 1988. Because our relationship was based on friendship and respect, and because we had dated for so long, I knew Kathy was God's choice for a mate. Now, after thirty years of marriage, I couldn't fathom doing life without her.

Up until this time, I'd always prayed for people going through medical challenges that God would help doctors make wise decisions. Our own two kids have serious medical issues, and I'd prayed for years for the correct medicines and the best doctors. But now, I turned solely to God for help. I realized for the first time in my life that God was the author of life, and He was the one who could save and sustain life.

The ambulance had already arrived by the time I got home. Kacey was standing outside the ambulance looking through the window. "Is Mom already in there?" I asked. Kacey just nodded, tears streaming down his face. I gripped his shoulder for a second to try to reassure him, and then raced to the back door of the ambulance and pounded on it. I needed to see my wife.

An EMT opened the door. Before he had it completely open, I told him I was Kathy's husband and wanted to see her. "I'm sorry, sir. You can't come inside the ambulance. It's too crowded, and we're trying to get your wife stabilized. We had to shock her heart a couple times to get it going. Even now, her heartbeat is weak." He told me they would leave for the hospital as soon as they got her stabilized. I felt frantic and helpless, not being able to see her.

After the EMT dismissed me, I walked into the house to find Kelsha kneeling on the living room carpet, sobbing and praying aloud. "God, help us—we can't live without our mom. Please do something. Bring her back to life, please, Lord."

I'd never heard my daughter pray before. My heart squeezed with pride to witness her faith in God to help us. But I hated that it took this horrible situation to bring it about.

Heavenly Adventures

I found myself barefoot in a large grassy field. A huge mountain range with one prominent mountain in the center stood before me, but at a distance.

I moved forward in the grass toward the mountain. It seemed odd to me that my feet never touched the ground, even though they were touching the grass. I felt like I was floating.

The mountain in the middle appeared to have snow on its peak. But the closer I came, the more I realized the glowing white covering was a blanket of diamonds. This mountain was also covered with flowering trees of every color blossom: bright orange, deep blue, rich violet. All of them blended together to form a patchwork of deep, vibrant color. I was drawn to this mountain. I felt power emanating from it, calling to my soul.

As I moved forward through the grass, each blade seemingly hummed with a unique kind of music. There was no specific melody to its song, just a lovely symphony of notes blending together to praise the Lord. I looked down at my feet and noticed that the grass bounced back from where my feet had touched it, leaving no imprint. It burst and brimmed with life, a life that swirled around and about everything there.

Nearby, about fifty to sixty children played ball and jumped rope. No one fought over the toys or argued like kids normally do. They all played together, peaceful and joyous. I smiled as I watched them, so carefree and happy. The children were from every race and culture. Some had dark skin and hair, others were fair with blond hair. I instinctively knew what age each one was, as all kids in the same age group were the same size and build.

The kids' clothing flowed and moved with them as they jumped and ran. As the girls played, their dresses flared out from their bodies when they twirled around or reached for the ball. The boys wore loose-fitting pants and tunics with a V-neck and squared-off shoulders. All the garments were white. The children's clothing seemed as if it was pulsing with energy. The white was luminous, alive, as if even their clothes radiated with the joy that filled their hearts, that their joy couldn't be contained. The life coming from within each person was glowing, shimmering.

Apparently, the kids didn't need adult supervision, because no adults were there. The children played together like a huge family that loves and understands one another. In perfect harmony.

> *The children's clothing seemed as if it was pulsing with energy, as if their clothes radiated with the joy that filled their hearts.*

This place—which I now realized was heaven—burst with light, like a sunny day with no clouds. But there was no sun and it wasn't hot—the temperature was perfectly comfortable. I didn't see any streetlights or other means of illumination; I realized that the source of light was the love of God in everything and everyone, glowing from within their hearts.

It made me think of the Bible verse that says, "And the city has no need of sun or moon, for the glory of God illuminates the city, and the Lamb is its light" (Revelation 21:23, NLT). Although I didn't see God or Jesus, I felt Their presence giving life to everything and everyone there.

And then I saw one person who wasn't wearing white. My mom! Suddenly she stood beside me. Her face was the same as I remembered, but her body was different. "Oh, Mom," I said. "I've missed you so much!"

She hugged me tight. "I've missed you, too, Kathy."

Mom was wearing a pair of blue jeans rolled up several times around her ankles and a red-and-white-checked shirt. I remembered her wearing that same outfit when I was about twelve and my uncle took Mom and me fishing. Mom hadn't owned a pair of jeans, so she borrowed a pair from my uncle, who was much taller than she was. She'd had to roll up the cuffs so she could walk.

When she was alive, Mom never could have managed a cartwheel. Here she was lithe and agile.

"Look what I can do," she said, and performed a cartwheel. When she was alive, Mom never could have managed a cartwheel. Here she was lithe and agile. She was perfect. When I told her how surprised I was, she laughed and said, "I can do anything here. You try it. I remember when you were a girl, you used to do all kinds of gymnastics." At first I refused, saying that I might break my neck. But she kept after me, and finally I tried one. It came out perfect! *How did I do that?*

I was so excited to be with Mom—a healthy version of Mom.

"Mom, I want to see Grandma and Grandpa and all our other relatives who have died. Where are they?" I really wanted to see my grandparents and aunts and uncles who I instinctively knew were here too. Mom told me they were all fine, not to worry about them, that they were busy. "Let's take a walk," she said. "That will calm you down."

Floating alongside me, Mom led me to a river, where the water was transparent. Gorgeous trees similar to the blossoming trees I'd seen on the mountain lined the riverbank. But to my astonishment, these trees had no roots. Yet their branches and leaves pulsed with life and energy. And something was different about the river itself—instead of mud, the bottom was created from jewels. Rubies, diamonds, emeralds—gems of all shapes, sizes, and colors. Even the riverbank was composed of various gems. It was breathtaking. I stared in disbelief as Mom stepped into the river.

"Mom, I can't believe you're getting wet."

"Oh, I love to swim here, Kathy. I swim all the time." On earth, I never saw Mom in a bathing suit. She'd never want to get her feet muddy or wet, let alone swim. Yet here she was, splashing and laughing, urging me to come on in. And she hadn't even put on a bathing suit before getting wet.

I finally waded in. The water felt silky and smooth. Both Mom and I lay down in the water. I expected to feel the initial shock that happens when you wade into a stream or jump into a pool of cold water. But this water was warm and inviting, like a hot tub. It came up to our ears as we lay there on those gorgeous jewels that made up the river bottom. They weren't sharp on my back, but smooth and soft. And there was that music again, that humming noise that made me feel peaceful and serene, this time coming from the water. This lovely sound embraced me and made me feel loved and safe.

Just as I closed my eyes and started to relax, a splash hit my face. I turned and saw Mom sitting up, her head thrown back, laughing like a child. *Is this really my mom?* But before I could think more about it, another splash landed on my head and I heard that same joyful laugh from Mom's lips. I splashed back, and Mom and I proceeded to have a good old water fight, like the best friends I'd always wished we'd been.

A Childhood of Abandonment

My dad—an abusive alcoholic—left Mom, my brother, and me when I was three, so Mom was all I had. She worked at the cafeteria of our local hospital for minimum wage and managed to keep a roof over our heads and food on our table. For as long as I can remember, I was petrified that Mom would die and leave us kids alone in the world. I would get out of my bed at night and sneak into her bedroom. I'd lie there on her bed and just watch her breathe, to reassure myself that she was still alive. I'd prayed all my life that I'd never have to live without my mom.

Up until the last ten or twelve years of Mom's life, she and I hadn't been close. I was a compliant child, the one who did what Mom told me to do with no argument. Yet Mom favored my older brother, who defied her every request and was as addicted to alcohol and violence as Dad from the time he was in middle school. Because Mom didn't stick up for me when my brother abused me, I felt betrayed and abandoned. When I finally got up the courage to tell Mom how I felt, she gradually made an effort to treat me with respect. That's when we became closer and started spending more time together.

After Tom and I were married, we included Mom in all our activities. We took her out to dinner, to the movies, shopping, and to all her doctor appointments. Mom had many health problems, including diabetes. We were able to buy her a little one-bedroom house close to where we lived. If she called me for help, I could be at her house in a few minutes.

The day before Mom died—July 11, 1998—she had spent time at our house, helping me cook and prepare for the twins' second birthday party.

She had a cough, and I asked her if she wanted me to take her to the doctor. "No, it's just the typical summer allergies," she said. "I'll be fine."

But the next afternoon, I got a call from my brother. He had been at Mom's house that day, mowing her lawn. When he went inside to get a drink of water, he saw that Mom had passed out. He called me and shouted for me to come over right away. I rushed to Mom's house, leaving Kelsha and Kacey with Tom. Mom was lying in her recliner, her lips already blue. My brother and I gave her CPR, but it was too late. She was already gone.

I felt like I'd let Mom down. She depended on me, and I couldn't bring her back to life. My lifelong terror of dying early returned after Mom passed. My dad had abandoned our young family, leaving me with feelings of rejection and abandonment throughout my life. After the twins were born, I'd become obsessed with the fear of dying early, abandoning my own children.

My lifelong terror of dying early returned after Mom passed. I'd become obsessed with abandoning my children.

Both twins suffered with serious health problems. That's why they still lived at home at age twenty. How would they manage without me? Tom worked long hours. If I died, who would take care of the kids? These thoughts haunted me day and night in the months following Mom's death.

Even though I was an active Christian, I also had some doubts concerning my faith in Jesus. I'd attended church throughout my life, and in 2004 I decided to follow Jesus and be baptized. But my childhood issues of abandonment ran deep. I wondered at times: What if, when we died, we simply just blipped out of existence and that was the end of us?

Worse, what if God was keeping a record of our sins, and when we got to a certain number of sins, or did something too horrible, He took our names off His record book of those going to heaven? My own dad had abandoned our family. Could my heavenly Father be trusted to remain faithful to me, even though I'd let Him down again and again? I think many Christians have these kinds of doubts.

Tom's Story: In God's Hands

A few minutes later, the EMTs told us they were heading out. The twins and I jumped in the car and followed them to our local hospital. The doctor on call that night let me in to see her. She was not conscious. "She's in a comatose state," he said. He opened her eyelids, but there was no response. "We'd like to send your wife to a heart specialist in Terre Haute. Would that be all right with you, Mr. Shields?"

Terre Haute was a thirty-minute drive away. I didn't give it a second thought. When you're in a life-or-death crisis like this, you don't sit down with a notebook and pen and make a list of pros and cons. You act from your gut. "Sure, do whatever you think she needs."

The doctor said he'd get back to me when he'd made arrangements. The kids and I sat in the waiting room. Kelsha was still crying and paced nervously from one end of the waiting room to the other. Kacey watched her for five minutes and then said, "Kelsha, you have to calm down. You're making me nervous."

"I'm trying—I just don't know what to do with myself."

"Come sit over here next to me, Kelsha," I said. Just then the doctor walked in. We looked at him. I know I was hoping he'd say Kathy just suddenly woke up and was fine, and we could take her home. Instead, he told us they couldn't find anyone in Terre Haute who would take her. Was it okay if they took her to Carle Foundation Hospital in Urbana, a ninety-minute drive? They had hoped to airlift her by helicopter, but the wings were frozen, and thawing them would take longer than driving her in the ambulance. "Of course, of course," I said, the tension in my voice making me sound like an out-of-tune violin. "Just get her the help she needs, please."

While they prepared Kathy for the trip, we rushed home and gathered everything we thought we might need: clothes, books to read, heavy coats, and snacks. We had no idea how long we'd be in Urbana with Kathy.

When we returned to the hospital, they were loading her into the back of the ambulance. We sped behind them, their lights blaring. Although no one said, "We need to pray," my kids and I desperately pleaded for Kathy's life. Aloud. Something we'd never done before. I was

> *I could feel God's presence as we three joined in agreement that the Lord would spare Kathy.*

especially touched by Kacey's prayer. Kacey is a very private person who keeps his feelings locked inside a closet in his heart. He rarely shows emotion. He's so even-tempered it aggravates Kelsha at times. But this night, he opened up and said, "Dear God, please don't let my mom die. We need her." I could feel God's presence as we three joined in agreement that the Lord would spare Kathy.

For the first time that night as I listened to my kids pray, the tears came. I hated what our family was going through, but the closeness I felt with my kids at that moment was unlike any feeling I'd ever experienced. God was showing me how much we need each other. I was upset and anxious, of course. But more than that, my heart burst with an awareness of God's Spirit at work, prompting us to pray, showing us how intertwined our lives are. All of us praying and weeping together created a sense of holiness and power in the car.

By the time I'd found a parking spot at Carle, they'd moved Kathy from the ER to a room in intensive care. Dr. White, the physician in charge of ICU, told me that they'd had some trouble in the ambulance on the way and had to apply the paddles to Kathy again. They had also inserted an oxygen tube into her lungs to help her continue to breathe.

All the nurses in the ICU told me that Kathy was in good hands with Dr. White. Carle is a teaching hospital, and Dr. White had been an instructor at one time. She asked a ton of questions and told us she suspected Kathy had aspirated some pills she took while she sat at the kitchen table talking with Kelsha earlier that evening.

"Right now we're not seeing any activity in your wife's brain," she said, her voice filled with compassion. "But we'll continue to monitor it and let you know if anything changes."

Taking a deep breath, I gathered all my courage and asked, "So what's it look like, Doc?"

"Mr. Shields, I just don't want you to get your hopes up that Kathy will fully recover from this episode and be the same person she was before this happened. We are doing everything possible to help her come out of it, but I have to be honest. You may need to prepare yourself to make some hard decisions."

My heart sank at her words. *If there was no activity in Kathy's brain, did that mean they were simply keeping her alive with their machines? Even if she eventually woke up, would she not function completely? What would be needed to care for her once we got her home?* I tried to push those discouraging thoughts to the back of my brain and simply deal with what we could do right this minute. "Can we stay with her tonight?" I said.

The hospital would allow only one person to stay in the room with Kathy. A nurse showed the kids where the waiting room was, and they gave me a hug and said good night. By this time it was 3:00 on Monday morning. I didn't sleep a minute; I just prayed and begged God for Kathy's life and health for the next few hours.

> *I didn't sleep a minute; I just prayed and begged God for Kathy's life and health.*

Every couple hours a nurse came into the room and did what they called "breathing treatment," where a machine was used to get all the fluid out of her lungs through a tube in her nose. We wanted to make sure someone was with her at all times, but boy, was it hard to watch her body jerk when she coughed up that fluid, and then to see how hard she fought the nurse, trying to take the tube out. Because of this, Kathy was given a shot each time to sedate her. The twins and I tried to soothe her. "It's okay. They're trying to help you get better," we said. Even though Kathy wasn't conscious, we believed she could hear us.

She'd developed pneumonia along with a high fever. Dr. White wanted to do an EEG (a test to determine brain activity), but they had to wait until her fever went down. In addition to giving her the breathing treatments, the nurses had laid ice blankets on and around her to lower her temperature. I was glad she wasn't awake. I couldn't imagine how uncomfortable that must feel.

Kathy's Mystery Man in the Hospital

I cracked my eyes open and peeked out at a murky green wall, a picture window with the shades drawn, and a vinyl recliner. I tried to turn my head, but it was too heavy. My entire body felt weighted down, as if a bear was sitting on me. *Why is it so dark in here? Where am I?* This was not my bedroom or even my sofa. I realized I was in a hospital bed and had a tube running into my nose, an IV inserted into my arm, and a heart monitor stuck on my chest. *What is going on?* I thought. Fear shot through every atom of my being.

> The man smiled and began to answer my unspoken questions with thought messages.

Then I saw the stranger. Sitting cross-legged on the red tote marked "Caution: Biohazard Material" was a man I didn't recognize. Yet he seemed familiar to me in a subconscious way. Deep brown eyes and a long, slender nose were his most prominent features. Dark, wavy hair barely touched his shoulders. He wore sandals, tan cargo shorts, and a white tunic that glowed brighter than any light I'd ever seen.

I thought, *Oh, that shirt. It's beautiful. I wonder what makes it glow. It's as if it's alive.*

The man smiled, gentle and warm, and began to answer my unspoken questions with thought messages. He had the kindest, most reassuring voice I'd ever heard. *This garment is a reflection of my love for you and all my children.* His words wrapped around my heart and calmed me. *Don't be afraid, Kathy.* He knew my name! How can this be? *Your family is in the room with you. They've been here 24/7, ever since you arrived yesterday in the wee hours.*

I opened my eyes wider and strained to see my husband, Tom, and my twenty-year-old twins, Kelsha and Kacey. All of them had tears streaming down their cheeks, but they were grinning and laughing. *Why is my family crying and laughing? What are all these tubes in me?*

Every inch of my body, inside and out, screamed in pain. When I saw all the tubes and needles, I started yanking them out, telling Tom I needed to get home. Instead of helping me get free, Tom shouted for help. Nurses and doctors filled the tiny room, holding me down to keep me from disconnecting my IVs, feeding tube, and respirator. "Get them off of me, Tom," I shouted. "Do something!"

"Honey, you have to be still," said Tom, his voice breaking with sobs. "These tubes are helping you stay alive." With the greatest effort I turned my head a few inches and looked into Tom's deep brown eyes. Where there was usually kindness, terror and anguish shone. I knew I was in trouble. In the thirty years Tom and I had been married, he'd rarely shown fear.

The brown-skinned man across the room caught my eye and smiled at me. Waves of love emanated from him and washed over my body, like warm honey. *Don't be afraid, Kathy. I will stay here with you every minute. Rest and be still.* I began to relax and soon fell asleep.

Kelsha's Story: Mom's Special Man

Mom's temperature was so high that they packed her in ice blankets for two days. They did breathing treatments on her several times a day. They also had to induce a coma, since she had gone without oxygen for thirty minutes, and her body was still trying to "catch up" with itself now that she was breathing on her own. A nurse told me the drug they used to induce the coma was the same drug Michael Jackson had overdosed on and died from. I wasn't thrilled to hear that.

Because the hospital was short on the drug that kept Mom under, she sort of woke up—a dazed kind of awake—several times during those first few days in the hospital. Each time, she'd try to pull all the tubes out and scream that they were trying to keep her there against her will. She was confused and afraid. You could see the fear in her eyes. We tried to tell her that all these people were helping her, trying to keep her alive, but she didn't believe us.

I knew Mom had some weird stuff going on in her brain, but would she continue to see this "special man"?

During the first episode of her semi-awake states, I walked across her room and sat down on a red hazardous material bin. "Don't sit on my special man," Mom said. "He's sitting there, and he's been talking to me every time I wake up." Then she explained that he didn't actually talk. They communicated with each other by thoughts. If she thought something, he knew what she was thinking and answered her with his own thoughts. She was concerned that I'd sit on him and he'd leave the room. His presence seemed to comfort her.

"Okaaaaay," I said, and got up to move to a chair. I looked at Dad to see if he heard. He just glanced back at me, a blank look on his face, and shrugged. I knew Mom had some weird stuff going on in her brain and wasn't fully awake yet, but I never thought hallucinations would be part of her recovery process. Would she continue to see this "special man," as she called him? Who was he? A guardian angel? Someone from her past? Jesus?

Tom's Story: Holy Boldness

That first night at Carle was the longest night of my life. I read my Bible app and prayed all night long, just looking at Kathy and talking to God. During one of those times, as I sat and stared at my wife's closed eyes and still body, I realized how little control I had over this situation. I thought, *I'm not in control like I've always thought. God is.* And with that realization I was able to relax a bit.

I knew God loved Kathy—all of us—more than we could imagine. Since He was in control, I could trust Him to make the best decision possible for our family. Although doubt and fear attacked my mind during those dark hours, they were the most precious times with God I'd ever had. I felt His presence and nearness in the room with me and Kathy. Little did I know that Kathy was actually seeing Jesus each time she awoke and was having conversations with Him.

On Tuesday, Dr. White came in and repeated what she'd said the day before. "It looks about the same. Please don't get your hopes up."

At those words, something stood up inside me—a holy boldness—and I said, "No. She'll be all right." The doctor told me Kathy might have a lot of brain damage, after not breathing for over thirty minutes. She predicted that Kathy would need to live in a rehabilitation center for a time after she fully woke up, so she could learn to do everyday things like dress, eat, and drive.

That powerful word, "no," rolled out of my mouth again and I spoke with certainty. "God is watching over her." The doctor just looked at me and shook her head. I told her she was doing a good job and thanked her for all she'd done. I knew Kathy was in good hands with Dr. White, as all the nurses had told me. But I also believed she was in Jesus's hands, which is the best place she could be. I remembered I'd read a scripture once that said, "Can a mother forget her nursing child? Can she feel no love for the child she has borne? But even if that were possible, I would not forget you! See, I have written your name on the palms of my hands" (Isaiah 49:15–16, NLT). My faith grew bigger and stronger each time I told the Lord, "She's in Your hands."

Later that day I called to activate our church's prayer chain, a group of people who pray during an emergency and who call the next person on the chain to relay the message. Our congregation is small, but we believe in the power of agreement that Jesus taught us in Matthew 18:19–20 (MSG): "I mean this. When two of you get together on anything at all on earth and make a prayer of it, my Father in heaven goes into action. And when two or three of you are together because of me, you can be sure that I'll be there."

I also called our pastor, Kevin Levellie, to let him know what was happening and asked him to pray. That afternoon he showed up to pray with us and be with us. I breathed a sigh of relief and thought, *Thank You, God. Everything is going to be all right now.* I was so happy to see him, and I hugged him so hard I thought I might have broken a couple of his ribs. Kevin prayed a simple yet powerful prayer over Kathy: "Lord, take control of this situation and heal Kathy, in the name of Your Son, Jesus." It didn't take long, but we believed God answered us, and we thanked Him in advance.

Due to a hurricane in the country where the sedative that was being used on Kathy was manufactured, the hospital had to ration what was on hand. At night the beeper alerted us that Kathy's medicine was getting low. When that happened, she'd start to wake up. Not a good thing. She flailed her arms, tried to get out of bed, and shouted at everyone that she was being held against her will. Finally she had to be strapped down to keep her in bed. It took several nurses, both kids, and me half an hour or more to calm her down each time this happened. At the end of each episode like this, she'd calm down all of a sudden, as if someone else was in the room, reassuring her that all would be well.

When she was in this semi-awake state, she often talked about her "special man" who would communicate with her via thoughts. We figured she was hallucinating due to all the drugs going into her system. I was a bit worried about it but tried not to dwell on it. If seeing this man—whoever he was—helped Kathy cope, I'd go along with it.

At the end of each episode, she'd calm down all of a sudden, as if someone else was in the room, reassuring her that all would be well.

A few days later, they performed the EEG test on Kathy. "It didn't show any brain damage," Dr. White said, "but we won't know until we allow her to fully wake up and see if she recognizes you and how much she's able to care for her own needs." I knew Dr. White was trying to prepare me for the worst. But I refused to buy into that negative report. I kept telling everyone, "When they take her off the breathing machine and let her wake up, it's gonna be great."

That night, Jessica, my oldest daughter from a previous relationship, visited Kathy. Although Kathy didn't raise Jessica, the two are very close. Up until this time, Kathy hadn't responded to anyone's voice or touch, apart from having a panic attack when she was in a semi-awake state. I talked to Kathy day and night, assuring her that I was there beside her. "You're gonna be fine, babe." She never moved or showed any signs of recognizing my voice. But when Jessica stood next to her and said, "Hey, Kathy, it's Jess," Kathy moved her head toward Jess's voice. I thanked God over and over that there was some activity going on. Little did we know *how much* Kathy could see, hear, and sense during that twelve-day period.

Back in Heaven

When we tired of our water fight game, Mom and I stood to get out of the jewel-bottom river. The minute I stood up, my hair, my clothes, my body were completely dry. It didn't take a second. It was instantaneous. It was as if I had never been wet.

All the colors in heaven are deeper, more vibrant than the colors on earth, which are dull and flat compared to the heavenly hues.

Mom turned to me. "It's time for you to go now, Kathy." Her eyes were soft and kind. We then walked over to a circle of brilliant pink tulips planted in dark, almost black, rich soil. I say brilliant because all the colors in heaven are deeper, more vibrant than the colors on earth, which are dull and flat compared to the heavenly hues. Mom plucked a single tulip and tucked it behind my ear, as if she was giving me a going-away gift.

"Mom, I just got here. I don't want to leave," I said. I was starting to feel a little upset, kind of frustrated, like a five-year-old who doesn't get her way. But there are no tears in heaven. I wanted to pitch a fit, but I couldn't make myself.

The tulip tickled my neck, so I reached to take it out of my hair. I held it up to my ear then and, just as with a seashell, I could hear the rushing of ocean waves in that tulip. Just like everything else in heaven, the tulip was singing and pulsing with life.

I handed the tulip back to Mom. She bent to stick it in the soil, and in its place, another tulip had sprouted and bloomed, just in the few seconds I'd had that first one in my hair. Mom placed the tulip back in the soil. She kind of wiggled it into the ground, and down it went, like you'd see in a cartoon. It rerooted itself in an instant. The leaves popped out of it just as if it had never left its place with the others. Flowers, like people, live forever in heaven.

I repeated what I'd told Mom a few minutes before—or was it an hour? There was no sense of time in heaven. "I want to stay here with you, Mom. I've never felt this whole and at peace before."

Mom's voice was kind and sweet, but firm. "Kathy, this isn't your time to live here yet. That time is coming very soon. But in the meantime, we are working on your house."

"Oh, Mom, you don't have to build me a home. You know I don't need anything big or luxurious." I'd forgotten Jesus's promise in John 14:2 (GNT): "There are many rooms in my Father's house, and I am going to prepare a place for you."

For the last thirty years, Tom and I had always lived in small houses, with barely enough room for us, our twins, and our many possessions. Although we owned several rental properties, we never had the desire to upsize our own home. Having a huge house wasn't important to us. As long as we had each other, we were content.

"I know you don't like fancy," said Mom. "We know exactly what your tastes are, and your house is going to have everything you like." More than once, I'd shared with Mom what my dream home would look like. Out in the country. Log home with plenty of room, especially a large kitchen and living room. Less stuff. Big front porch overlooking the mountains. With a pure creek running by it.

Mom assured me that the house they were building me would be exactly what I'd always dreamed. "You'll love it," she said with a huge grin.

Mom's tone now changed to serious. "Kathy, it's time for you to go. There is more work for you to do on earth. Your family needs you. But before you leave, I want you to know how beautiful I think you are. I love you and I am so proud of you and your family. Tom is a wonderful husband and dad, and you've done a tremendous job with the twins."

"Oh, Mom, if you could only see the twins now. They're so grown up and mature. And they love the Lord with all their hearts."

"I see them every day, honey, and you've done a great job raising them."

Words every mother longs to hear from their own mother, or anyone. But in my case, Mom's pride in me filled my heart to overflowing. Although she showed her love to me in a thousand little ways while I was growing up, I don't remember her saying, "I love you. I'm proud of you."

Tom's Story: She Knows Who We Are

Eight days after Kathy was admitted to the hospital, the doctor took out the oxygen tube to see if she could breathe on her own. I was gone from the room for a few minutes, and when I came back, she was fully awake.

Kathy asked about her mom. We told her that her mom had died several years earlier. Then she said, "Where's that guy?" We asked her what guy she was talking about. "The man who's been here with me the whole time. Can't you see him, sitting there on that red tote?"

The twins and I looked at each other and shrugged. "What's he doing?" I said.

"Nothing. He's just sitting there, watching me, like he has been doing the whole time I've been here." I knew that the man had to be Jesus.

I thought back to all those nights she woke up in a panic, ripping the tubes out of her nose and arms. I kept telling her, "It's going to be okay, Kathy." Now I realized it was the Spirit of God who calmed her down, not my words or the sedative they gave her. Jesus was the one who put her back to sleep every time.

> *I realized it was the Spirit of God who calmed her down, not my words or the sedative they gave her.*

We were supposed to tell the nurse when Kathy woke up, but we delayed telling anyone because we wanted to talk with her alone. I asked her if she knew what day and year it was. She said, "Is it 1979?" Kelsha and I looked at each other and both of us raised our eyebrows at once. I was tempted to panic, since Dr. White had warned me that Kathy might not be herself when she woke up, if ever. But then I asked her if she knew her name. "I know what my name is, Tom! Why are you asking me all these stupid questions?" When I heard that sass, I knew she was going to fully recover. With all she'd been through, the fight had never gone out of her.

While we chatted with Kathy, a nurse came in. "Oh my goodness, she's awake." The nurse grabbed Kathy's chart and started asking her all the same questions we'd asked. I could tell Kathy's patience was starting to wear thin at all of us wanting to know such obvious facts. The twins and I left the room to go get something to eat, telling Kathy we'd be back shortly. The nurse finally hung up Kathy's chart again and left, too, so Kathy could rest.

When we got back from our lunch, a cognition therapist came to visit Kathy. She asked her a lot of questions in an attempt to discover how accurate Kathy's perceptions were. Kathy struggled to answer all of the therapist's questions. Finally the lady said, "There is something there that's hindering her thought processes, even though it doesn't show up on the EEG."

> The fact that she recognized her family was huge. I didn't care that she couldn't do those math problems they were throwing at her.

"I'm just happy she knows us," I said, my voice cracking as tears welled in my eyes. To me, the fact that she recognized her family was huge. I didn't care that she couldn't do all those math problems they were throwing at her. But they warned me that she'd need to go into a rehab center before she could live at home. The doctor refused to release her to our care.

I asked if they could at least have her do therapy in Paris, so we could take her to her appointments. The doctor said he'd look into it. I decided to take matters into my own hands and call the hospital in Paris to see if they'd give Kathy physical rehab, and explained all the different things the doctor had told me she needed. The physical therapist in Paris assured me that they could provide all the therapy my wife needed. When I told the cardiologist, he seemed surprised, but called and made arrangements for her PT appointments there.

Return of the Mystery Man

I spent a few more days in the hospital. One morning, the cardiologist recommended that I have a defibrillator implanted, a battery-powered device that shocks the heart if it goes into cardiac arrest. One person referred to this device as "the guardian angel standing nearby to keep you safe if your heartbeat becomes irregular." The surgery would take around ninety minutes. I'd have to have that device inside me for the rest of my life.

Tom and the kids agreed that I needed a defibrillator to prevent any future heart attacks. I didn't want one. I believe that Jesus is our healer, and I put my trust in Him, not doctors and their methods. But my family had had such a horrible scare when I passed out and almost didn't come back. I hated the thought of putting my loved ones through that nightmare another time. So I reluctantly signed the papers.

Friday, January 19, three different doctors came into my room around 7 a.m. and explained the surgery to Tom and me in terms we could understand. "We call this device an ICD, which stands for an Implantable Cardiac Device. We will slit a muscle just below the skin to create a pouch in Kathy's chest, right below her collarbone on the left side. After that, we'll insert a battery-powered pulse generator into the pouch. The generator is about the same diameter as the face of a pocket watch. Wires that run from the pulse generator to the surface of the heart are installed through blood vessels. If your heart stops beating, this device will shock it, so that it starts up again. We will also install a pacemaker at the same time, to regulate your heartbeat. With this method, we won't need to perform open-heart surgery."

I was relieved at the news I wouldn't need open-heart surgery. Yet I still resisted the idea of having anything foreign inserted into my body. But I'd already signed the papers. What could I do?

When the medical assistant came to wheel me down to the surgery, I started yelling at him. "I don't want this gadget in my chest! Unstrap me and let me up!" I tried to grab the doors of the elevator to keep it from closing. Suddenly, the man wearing the glowing tunic appeared at my side.

> *Suddenly, the man wearing the glowing tunic appeared at my side. He spoke through our minds, just as he did before.*

"Kathy, it's okay. Calm down and let go of the doors." He spoke through our minds, just as he did before.

When I started to answer the man, the orderly said, "Why don't you want this surgery?"

"I'm not talking to you," I shouted. A curious look came into his eyes. I turned my head to say something else to the glowing man, but he swiveled and walked through the wall. *Oh no, I've upset him by yelling.* I began to bawl, and hollered after him, "Please come back. I want to talk to you."

Although the orderly still thought I was talking to him, I ignored him and spoke to the man. "I'm sorry for yelling like that. I thought you'd left, and it scared me."

He said, "Oh, honey. I didn't go away. I have never left you." He then told me it was necessary to have the surgery done, and to cooperate with the medical team that was trying to help me. He gazed at me, his dark brown eyes intense and brimming with affection. "I love you, Kathy. I'm always with you, even when you can't see or hear me."

Hounding God for Answers

Every day for three months after I came home from the hospital, I hounded God. "Why am I here, Lord?" "Is there something special You want me to do?" "I don't know why I didn't die; all my doctors said my recovery was a miracle." Day after day I questioned God, urging Him to give me answers.

When Tom would come home from work to find me still in bed, too depressed even to get up and dress, he'd sit down beside me and ask, "What's wrong, honey?"

"I don't know, Tom. I'm just not satisfied with my life anymore. I can't even figure out why I'm not happy. I beat death. All the doctors say I'm a miracle. Yet I have this heavy feeling in the pit of my stomach, a dissatisfaction I've never felt before. Like there's something more for me to do, some divine calling, but I can't get God to tell me what it is."

Seeing the Man Again

After being home from the hospital for a month, all the restrictions the doctor gave me were making me feel like a prisoner in my own home. No driving. No lifting my arms above my head. No strenuous exercise. My family treated me as if I were a frail ninety-year-old—or a toddler. "Don't climb on that chair, Mom—let me change the light bulb." "I'll put the clean dishes away, Mom—you shouldn't be reaching into the high cupboards."

Finally, I'd had enough. One afternoon when Tom and Kelsha were both at work and Kacey was playing an online game, I decided to sneak out. I quietly lifted the car keys from the hook on the kitchen wall, grasped them tight so they wouldn't jangle, and tucked them into my purse. "Kacey, I'm going out for a minute," I said. "I'll be back soon." Kacey was so engrossed in his game, he barely mumbled "Okay." I tiptoed out the door and started the car as quietly as I could, then drove to a thrift store about a mile from our house. I felt like I was a bird escaping from a tiny, restrictive cage.

At the thrift store, I snuck to the back corner where I knew there were four shelves of books. *Perhaps if I find something entertaining to read, I won't go totally stir crazy.* I placed a shopping basket in front of me to hide behind, so no one who knew me would question what I was doing out of the house. After fifteen minutes or two hours—my awareness of time vanished—a tiny face leaped out at me from the spine of a book titled *The Jesus I Never Knew* by Philip Yancey. That half-inch-wide face was the man in my hospital room! I could see only his piercing dark eyes and prominent nose in that picture on the spine. Yet I knew it was the same guy. Not a guardian angel as I had thought. He was Jesus.

> My trip to heaven erased any doubts I had about God.

My whole body shook with joy. I rushed to the counter and paid for the book. I still have it. It sits on my counter in the kitchen, where I spend most of my time.

My trip to heaven erased any doubts I had about God. When I saw Mom and she showed me the glorious beauty of heaven and told me what I had to look forward to when my time came, that lifetime of fear vanished. I knew that if I believe in Jesus and give my life to Him, then that peaceful, joy-filled place is where I will go when I die. No one had to tell me; my heart simply knew by the overwhelming feeling of peace I experienced there. God's love for all His children is so much larger than any of us can imagine.

My Life since My Near-Death Experience

Kathy Shields

Six different doctors have told me I am a walking miracle. They explained that in most cases, it takes only three to four minutes of no oxygen going to the brain to cause permanent damage. I had no oxygen for thirty minutes. I know it is because of Jesus that I am here today, full of love and promise for the life in front of me.

Q *In what way has your life changed since your NDE?*

A This experience has caused me to value my family more. After my love for Jesus, my husband and kids mean everything to me.

I also don't worry as much as I used to about how tidy and neat my house is. If the kids need to talk, I drop what I'm doing and listen and talk to them. The dishes and dust will still be there in an hour. My relationship with Tom, Kelsha, and Kacey far outweigh the importance of having the perfect house.

Q *How did your NDE change your relationship with God?*

A I thought I loved Jesus before I saw Him with my own eyes and talked to Him, but now I have this intimacy with Him that I never thought possible.

I love to read the Bible, and I understand it better now than I did before my NDE. It's like a puzzle. All the pieces fit together, and it's up to us to find their meaning and see how they fit into the scheme of history as well as our own life.

I believe everything we go through in life teaches us about love, forgiveness, compassion, and perseverance. This life prepares us for heaven.

Q *Did your experience change your family's relationship with God?*

A It did. As a family we've always talked about God, how He is always watching over us and caring about us. But my health scare caused all of us to thank God for the blessings He has given to us.

I am so grateful that my children know that God is deeply involved in all aspects of their lives and that He is in control.

In the Circle of Love

By Bryan Coleman, as told to Anita K. Palmer

------------ ◆ ------------

Above all, keep loving one another earnestly,
since love covers a multitude of sins.

1 Peter 4:8 (ESV)

I was dead. I believed I was. I was afraid I was.

I was in total darkness. It was utterly silent. Abruptly, a kind, deep voice surrounded me like a soft, warm blanket. It asked a simple question: "Do you want to see what happened to you?"

I saw no beings to reply to, but I answered "yes." I'm not sure if I spoke the word or thought it.

Immediately, images came at me like video clips.

Coming Up Short

I had come home from running errands on Saturday afternoon, November 9, 2013. If you know anything about Houston, the city where I live, you know the temperatures in late fall can be as warm as eighty or as cool as sixty. I remember only that the day was sunny and pretty.

My landscaper had finished trimming the bushes and cutting the lawn. After I paid him and said goodbye, I noticed that the gutters were not cleaned. So, despite being sixty-five years old and having undergone at that point more than half a dozen back surgeries since my thirties, I decided I'd do it myself. I can be stubborn that way.

I live by myself in a two-story colonial-style house in The Woodland Heights, my city's oldest residential neighborhood. A long time ago, residents could reach downtown on a horse in five minutes or less. These days, it is part of the residential district known as Greater Heights.

My yard's outside water spigot is on the side of the house, about halfway between the front and the back. In my backyard, I kept four fifteen-foot hoses connected in one long length and rolled up on a reel. That combination allowed me to reach any part of my backyard and take care of things the sprinkler system didn't reach. The drawback of keeping the hose lengths connected on one reel is not being able to visually detect if someone has removed any of them.

Things would have turned out differently if I'd thought of checking for that.

> I climbed the rungs up to where a little sign says "Do Not Climb above This Point." I admit I did not obey the sign.

I grabbed a ten-foot lightweight aluminum ladder from the garage, which is at the rear of my house, and unfolded it at the roofline of the garage. Then I pulled out enough hose from the reel to reach the ladder, plus a little extra. After turning the water on full blast, I climbed the rungs—up to where a little sign says "Do Not Climb above This Point." Yes, I admit I did not obey the sign.

I was blasting away with a high-pressure nozzle, feeling good in the sparkling sunlight to be getting the job done efficiently—until I reached about three-quarters of the way down the length of the garage. That's when I tugged on the hose to lengthen it, and it didn't budge. I figured it was kinked or caught on something. So I gave it a hard, two-arm yank.

A Warm Voice

What I've just described are my memories of what transpired up to this point. The next thing I can recall was the darkness—and the voice. A warm, inviting, masculine-sounding voice. Whether it was audible or in my consciousness, I cannot say.

Then the question. "Do you want to see what happened to you?" As soon as I responded, I saw what I would describe as a vision. It showed the ladder tipping and thundering down fast like a tree toppling in a forest. I watched as my body flew outward for about ten feet in an arc, projecting off the ladder's top and twisting in midair. I saw the back of my head smack the dry, hard lawn. My six-foot body bounced once and then lay perfectly still.

Then I heard the all-encompassing voice ask a second question: "Is there anyone there that you need to take care of?"

I have a son and a daughter, Doug and Sarah, both of whom are independent adults. They immediately came to mind. "My children," I responded.

The voice replied, "You do not need to worry about your children. They will be more than adequately taken care of."

I knew that my children would be taken care of financially because of my many years as a successful attorney. But the impression I got during this exchange concerned being their father, that they would not need my parenting anymore. I didn't know quite how to comprehend that, and I still don't. At that moment, I, for the first time, seriously considered the implication of the fact that I was dead.

I was suddenly filled with fear and helplessness. I was terrified of being dead. There certainly were a lot of ways I could have died that would be worse than falling off a ladder. It was quick and done. But all I was thinking about right then was, *I am dead. I am dead.*

I was not going to be able to do anything else in life. My remaining hopes and dreams weren't going to be fulfilled. I was not sure, despite what the nice voice said, that my children would be okay. But the most terrifying thing was knowing that I had not always lived the Christian life as I should have.

I was brought up in a very religious family, so I knew that I had not always done the things I had been taught to do. I did not pray as often as I should have. I did not go to church as often as I should have, even though I taught a Sunday school class for many years. Most important, I did not always live my life for God.

I did not know what was going to happen to me. I could imagine a lot of things, most of which were not pleasant.

Enwrapped by Love

What I remember next was the strange, growing light. It's hard to describe because I have never seen a light like it. It was so bright that I felt that if I looked at the source, even though I could not see any source, I might be blinded.

I didn't ascribe any meaning to the light at this point. I had little knowledge of near-death experiences (NDEs). I had heard about them, but I hadn't studied them. I did not know that light often is understood to be love by those who have experienced an NDE.

Despite the prevalence of light, I still could not see the source of the voice addressing me. Nor could I see any other beings. That concerned me. But by this point, I realized whatever was happening was out of my control and I had no choice except to go with the flow, so to speak.

The nature of the bright light began to suggest kaleidoscopic auras, sort of like you see when you look at the surface of soap bubbles being blown by children. Then a distance away—I couldn't determine distance in this situation, but maybe the equivalent of twenty feet—a gigantic orb-like shape came into view. The lighted orb was so bright I could see nothing between it and me. Or perhaps I should say whatever "me" was there. The orb was opaque and had a colorful outer sheen that was

> *The orb was opaque and had a colorful outer sheen that was constantly moving, as if rainbows swam in its surface.*

constantly moving, as if rainbows swam in its surface. It looked big enough that a car could be driven into it.

Then the same kind, rich-sounding male voice returned and communicated, "Go into the bubble."

I was momentarily stumped. There was no obvious entrance. How could I comply?

And though I don't quite know how I got there, I found myself inside the giant bubble-like thing. The best way I can describe it is by comparing it to a planetarium that some large science museums have, where a giant domed ceiling acts as a screen. Viewers lean back, look up, and watch something projected onto the ceiling.

I looked around. What I saw next was very curious to me. The bubble was slightly hazy or misty. Even so, I could see ascending rows of seats encircling half of its exterior, like the audience of a theater-in-the-round. Human-looking figures sat in the seats. I don't know how many, but I would guess around fifty. I couldn't see any of them well enough to recognize anyone, and I couldn't tell what they individually looked like, but they definitely were people.

> *I have felt love for people. I have felt love for all sorts of thing. But this was a hundred times stronger.*

I had no idea who they were or why they were there. But then I began to feel an overwhelming love emanate from them. A love like I'd never felt before. It was so overpowering. I have felt love for people, for women, for my children. I felt love for all sorts of things. But this was a hundred times stronger. Something immeasurable. Every time I think of it, I start crying.

Because of that atmosphere of love, I presumed these people were friends and relatives who predeceased me. Or perhaps they were people I had helped during their lives. They were there for some reason. Perhaps they were to witness whatever was going to happen. If you want to know what I really thought, I supposed they might be there to lobby for me—for the final deposition of my soul.

They never said a word, though, and I had no interaction with them at all.

My view shifted toward the middle of the bubble, to an area that appeared to serve as a floor. I saw a large item there. Believe it or not, it was a recliner. A white La-Z-Boy–looking lounger right in the middle of the sphere. It seemed to be made of leather.

Then the voice said, "Please sit down and relax."

Think of that. A heavenly figure of some sort, courteously asking *me* to please sit down—and to relax.

So I did. Sit down, anyway. Relax, not so much. I was still scared, but I would have done anything He told me to do. I had already figured out He was a lot bigger deal than I was.

Then He said, "Let us take a look at your life."

Images of Kind Acts

At that comment, whatever feeling of relaxation I had developed evaporated and I stiffened with terror.

In over six decades of earthly life, the only commandment I was not confident that I had not broken was the seventh ("Do not kill anybody"). This included the two new commandments that Christ gave us while He was on earth. I had cheated, I had stolen, I had coveted. I had had multiple relationships that I should not have. I had not always loved my neighbors as myself. I had not always put God ahead of everything else in my life. If you wanted to write a litany of my sins, you'd need a bigger book than this one.

The thought hit me: *This is Judgment Day.* If so, I was not expecting constructive criticism. I was expecting condemnation.

I leaned back in the recliner. But I promise you I did not relax.

Looking up to the top of the bubble, I would estimate the height in earthly terms to be around twenty-five feet. The interior ceiling of the bubble was some sort of screen, like a gigantic television screen or a small movie screen. Then I began to see images somehow start flowing down from the top.

As the first one became visible I wasn't sure at first what I was seeing. Then I began to recognize a fresh and vivid memory. Just a few weeks prior, I had been driving home from work. Since my neighborhood is affluent, we have a lot of homeless people on street corners. Many are holding signs that say things like "Hungry," "Homeless," "Please Help," and so on.

I had stopped at the one red light between my house and my office. It was afternoon traffic, so there were a lot of vehicles stopped at the light, but I was close to the front of the line. I saw a guy standing there. He was obese, so I assumed he hadn't been hungry. I leaned out and asked, "Why are you homeless?"

"Because I am a junkie," he said.

"Do you want to be a junkie?" I asked.

"No!" he said. "But there is nothing I can do about it."

"Yes, there is," I said.

"What?" he asked.

During this time, I had been helping finance a drop-in recovery home, which we called the Twenty-Four-Hour Club because it never closes. It was a last-chance operation. If you were an addict, you could knock on the door, and if there was room, someone would let you in, help you detox, feed you, clothe you, counsel you, take care of you. You could stay until you were ready to go back out into the world.

Most of the people who lived there were really poor and had nowhere to go. One day when I left a meeting at the Club, I ran across a guy sitting on the front porch. He had on one shoe. I said, "Where is your other shoe?" He said, "I only found one." This man was indicative of the Club's clientele.

Back at that intersection that day, I gave the junkie a twenty-dollar bill and told him where the Twenty-Four-Hour Club was. I did not expect him to go. I assumed he would buy drugs with the money. The light changed and I drove away.

But in the heavenly snippet, I saw that he went. He got clean. He got sober. And his life was being changed forever. All because I stopped and did something good. Thinking about that makes me teary to this day.

That was just the very first clip. They were not "screening" in earthly real time. They came fast—*bang, bang, bang, bang, bang*—but somehow I was able to perceive the stories as if they were in real time. The images would last maybe a second and a half, and they might convey thirty human minutes. One after another, after another, after another. They kept coming.

The clips came fast. The images would last maybe a second and a half, and they might convey thirty human minutes.

All of them were good things I had done.

I recognized every single incident. And almost every one of them had consequences I had not realized had occurred.

Not a single episode showed me doing anything other than being kind and loving and generous and helpful. And I knew I had not behaved that way during the majority of my life.

In the middle of this story stream I spoke for the first time since entering the bubble.

"Where are the bad things I have done?" I asked.

The voice answered. He said, "God does not see those, for I took all of them for you."

That's when I realized that I was speaking with Christ Himself.

It Was All True

In the instant that I heard Christ say those words, I knew that everything would be okay, and I was filled with relief. That's when I truly relaxed. Christ had died for my sins, making them invisible to the heavenly Father. All my bad behavior was blotted out by Jesus.

There are no words to describe my awe. It was just amazing.

I had been brought up in a rather hellfire-and-brimstone-type Baptist church. All my life I dreaded death, because I was never comfortable with the idea that all my sin was just going to be forgotten. I anticipated I was going to die, and I was going to go to some place, and somebody was going to talk to me about the bad things I had done and the good things I had done, and tell me whether or not I got into heaven.

> *In this moment, I realized I wasn't being judged. I wasn't facing damnation.*

But in this moment, I realized I wasn't being judged. I wasn't facing damnation. Yes, I was left with the feeling that I should have done more to show God's love to others. But there was no settling of my debts. The debts had already been settled.

And because of that, all my fears were gone. All the Biblical teachings I had learned about the sacrifice of Christ on my account were true, permitting a wretched sinner like me to enter the kingdom of heaven.

I felt a happiness like I had never known, a peace beyond belief, and a contentment with my death that was indescribable. I was going to heaven!

My next line of thinking was, *When? How much longer?* I admit that I was hoping the scenario would soon dissolve and we could get on to wherever heaven was. I wanted to go out and talk to those people outside the bubble. I wanted to meet Jesus! I had so many questions!

But at that moment I felt my head bouncing up and down against a hard surface.

A heavy weight compressed my chest. Wuss, my 150-pound Rottweiler, was standing on me, licking my face. I became aware that I was flat on my back in the sunshine in my yard.

And that made me angry. I did not want to return to earthly life.

Changing Direction

I grew up in New Boston, a small town in the extreme northeast corner of Texas, near Texarkana. It's called the Four States Area, where Texas meets up with Oklahoma, Arkansas, and Louisiana. When I was a kid, there were about twenty-five hundred people living in New Boston, which was named not for the historic Massachusetts city but for a local shopkeeper. My high school graduating class consisted of seventy-two seniors.

I always knew God was in my life. I always prayed. My father believed in God but didn't attend church much. But my mother was in church every time the doors opened—and she brought me with her. Back then, kids who attended Sunday school fifty out of fifty-two Sundays in a year received what they called the Perfect Attendance Pin. Then the next year, if you made it to fifty Sundays, you got a gold laurel to put around the pin. Every year after that, you'd get a bar to attach to the pin.

I had a Perfect Attendance Pin that was nine yards long. That's an exaggeration, of course, but I was very active in the church as a child. Youth group, summer camps, everything. Of course, during my adolescent years I was, shall we say, less compliant. It was the era of exploration and rebellion, and after I got out from under my parents' authority, I did a lot of both.

The main thing New Boston was known for was being next to two US Army installations. They were where the majority of the population worked. Unless you were a town merchant or something like that, you were expected to go work at "the depot" all your life and then retire.

That's what my folks did. My father and two of my uncles had risen very high in the management ladder of the depot. My family had been sent for two-year assignments to France and Okinawa, and we traveled around Europe on vacations. But while my parents enjoyed the sights, all they wanted to do was go back to New Boston, Texas.

> *You were expected to go to work at "the depot" all your life and then retire. But I wanted to go to college.*

So when I told my parents I wanted to go to college, they thought I was crazy.

"Why? You can work at the depot," my father said. Because I was his son and my uncles' nephew, I would have had no problem moving up through the management chain and making something like a decent living. "You can have a good job your whole life. Your family all work out there. How can't you see that?"

But I insisted. "I want to go to college."

"Well, you'll have to pay for it," was my father's response.

And so I did. My parents couldn't have helped financially even if they wanted to. My father had been in a very bad train wreck by then and was disabled. They were living on disability and the small income my mother brought in from working at the credit union at the depot.

Even after I earned an associate's degree from Texarkana College and a bachelor's in business from the Stephen F. Austin State University, my father remained unsupportive of my spreading my wings. I know he loved me, but he just didn't get it. In fact, when I went to law school, he used to make jokes that he would rather find out I was in prison than that I was a lawyer.

My mother was emotionally supportive, though. She wanted me to do what I wanted to do. She would send me a little bit of money whenever she could.

After state university, I jumped right into an MBA program. Then I ran out of money. So I moved down to Houston for the summer to work and save.

That's where God intervened and set me on a new path. Only I didn't know it at the time.

Okay, You're In

Since I refused to lie in job interviews and claim I was in Houston for longer than the summer, no one wanted to hire me in positions related to my education. That's how I ended up working two low-wage jobs: one at a convenience store at night and another at a gas station during the day.

The station had a regular customer named Harold Farb. He has long since died, but back then Mr. Farb was a very wealthy, well-known real estate mogul in town. When he came into the station, he did not even give you a credit card. He and his whole crew just drove in and we pumped their gas, performed the expected cleaning and service, and wrote it down. Once a month, he would pay the whole balance.

In those days, service stations attendants, as they were called, washed customers' windshields and checked their oil while pumping their gas. On one day, Mr. Farb got out of the car and looked at me. He had never spoken to me before.

"How long have you been out of prison?" he asked.

"Mr. Farb, I have never been to prison," I said, a little shocked.

"Then what is a nice-looking, obviously educated young man like you doing working in a service station?"

I told him I was spending the summer working to save for graduate school. He asked what program I was in. I told him business.

"You don't want an MBA," he said. "Go to law school."

I had never given law as much as a single thought. Besides, as I pointed out to Mr. Farb, I hadn't done any of the typical preparations needed to apply, and here it was already July.

"Don't worry about that. Just go down to South Texas College of Law and say I said to let you in."

I thought he was loony. One, I had never heard of South Texas College of Law, and two, how could I just be "let in," anyway?

After Mr. Farb left, though, I began to think about it. Why didn't I check it out? What did I have to lose? You know how it is when you're young.

Actually, what I had to lose was the two dollars needed to pay for parking. I also had to borrow slacks and a jacket from my roommate. Blue jeans weren't going to cut it.

South Texas College of Law was at the time a little night law school in downtown Houston with courses taught by working attorneys. It occupied a small three-story building. When I told the woman at the front desk I was there to see the dean, she balked and said he only spoke to students by appointment. I told her I wasn't a student.

"I know this is going to sound crazy but a gentleman named Mr. Farb told me to come down here and tell the dean to let me into law school."

Without hesitating, she reached for her phone, got on the intercom, and said, "Harold Farb sent a young man down to see you."

"All right, send him in," came the reply.

> *Harold Farb didn't get me into law school. God did.*

I was stunned but also naïve. I couldn't imagine that this was the way things were done, but I didn't know.

When I sat down, the dean asked, "How do you know Mr. Farb?" I told him my story. Then he asked, "Did you go to college?"

I said yes.

"Okay," he said. "You're in."

I discovered later that Harold Farb was a member of the board of regents for South Texas College of Law, so the dean worked with him. But Harold Farb didn't get me into law school. God did.

God Connections

It was exciting to start a new program of study at a new institution. What wasn't exciting was the fact that tuition at South Texas was a great deal higher than it was for my old MBA program. I was living in a one-room apartment, surviving on canned mackerel (I will never eat mackerel again), and still I ran out of money a month into the term.

With my savings gone, I decided I had no choice but to drop out and go back to work. But God had different plans, again.

I went to an employment agency near where I lived. "Why are you dropping out of law school?" asked the gentleman doing the interview. He seemed to actually care.

I rattled off the reasons. "Because I can't afford to go. I can't pay my tuition. I can't eat. I mean, I have lost like forty pounds and we're not halfway through the semester."

"Well, I may have a job for you. There is a firm in Houston called Fulbright Crooker Freeman Bates & Jaworski. They are looking for a law clerk. If you would like, I will set up an interview for you," he said.

Of course I said yes.

Being a country boy, I assumed the firm's name meant they had five lawyers. No. Fulbright Crooker Freeman Bates & Jaworski was the largest law firm west of the Mississippi River. The Jaworski in the name was Leon Jaworski, the president of the American Bar Association. The same year in which I would graduate from South Texas College of Law, Mr. Jaworski would become famous for being tapped to serve as a special prosecutor during the Watergate scandal.

The firm's offices were on multiple floors, and they were big and fancy. I had an appointment with a Mr. Talbot. To reach his office, I had to walk down a hall that was bigger than my entire law school.

The interview did not start well. Mr. Talbot asked what school I was attending. When I replied, he said, "We do not hire people from South Texas."

"Why?" I asked, my heart sinking.

"We do not consider it to be a law school. Why did you come here?"

"An employment agency sent me," I said.

"Well, we have never hired anyone from South Texas College of Law for anything. We do not even let them work in our mailroom."

"Mr. Talbot, I am starving to death," I blurted out. I didn't have anything to lose. "I do not care what job you give me. I will sweep the floors if you want me to. I will clean the bathrooms if you want me to."

I guess he felt sorry for me, because he paused and then said, "I am going to give you a chance."

At first no one spoke to me or even looked me in the eye. The cold shoulders continued for months. Gradually, though, people began to like me. I made friends with young lawyers there, hot shots from Ivy League schools.

At first no one spoke to me or looked me in the eye. Gradually, though, people began to like me.

Somewhere during this time an older lawyer came to me. He was a great guy. He asked me, "When you graduate, would you like to come to work with me?" I liked him a lot. We had the same birthday. So I said yes.

After graduation, I took the Texas State Bar exam and scored ninety-one—the top score for the entire state. I only mention that because all of a sudden, I was not this backwater South Texas College of Law night-school kid who didn't know anything. I had beaten all the Harvard, Yale, and Princeton grads, and people began to notice me.

You're in the Army Now

Before this, during my first semester in law school, things got complicated when I received a draft notice. I started to lament about all the sacrifices I'd made for naught because now I was faced with going to the Vietnam War as a private in the US Army. A fellow law student sitting with me stopped me. He told me I could get a deferment by joining ROTC. I eventually would have to go active duty as an officer, but I could continue my schooling in the meantime. So that's what I did.

After graduation, a while after the older man and I started the new law practice, it became time to enter active duty. I didn't want to leave Houston to be a second lieutenant in the ordnance corps at Aberdeen Proving Ground in Maryland. But I went.

> *The military had realized I was a lawyer and assigned me to help train new army attorneys.*

Of my eight years in the Army Reserves, two were active duty. The army can recall you anytime they need to, and that happened to me several times, making it a challenge to run a law practice.

One time was a God thing, I now see. I got recalled and sent to Fort Sam Houston in Texas. I couldn't figure it out. There is no ordnance corps there. But then I discovered I'd been ordered to the Judge Advocate General's Office. The military had realized I was a lawyer and assigned me to help train a dozen or so new army attorneys.

The army liked what I did and wanted me to do a branch transfer into the JAG. But that meant I would have had to agree to stay for another four years. That wasn't possible. I had a private practice to return to. I got out.

In my late thirties, I married. Unfortunately, after nine years of marriage, my wife left me and our young son and daughter, Doug and Sarah. By then, I was making enough money that I could afford a nanny during the day. I took the kids to school every morning on the way to work and was home for them in the evenings. We attended church every week, and I also taught Sunday school. I coached Doug's and Sarah's sports teams. I was even a Brownie "mom." Being a single parent was hard, but I did what I had to do.

Looking back, I realize all these connections and achievements were the hand of God. God wanted me to have a career in law. He was taking care of me and my family. But I did not recognize that at that time. I thought I was just experiencing a strange bunch of coincidences. I didn't believe God swooped down and removed the obstacles in our lives. I felt as if it was up to me to get by one day at a time, and I was determined to succeed.

In fact, I felt I didn't deserve anything special. I probably deserved God's condemnation. And I spent most of my adult life trying to ignore that sensibility.

Back on Earth

I have read reports by people who have had near-death experiences who describe returning to earth and feeling overwhelmed with anger and disappointment. They are crushed by having to leave behind an all-engulfing peace and love and return to overwhelming problems and limitations.

I have to admit that in the instant I realized I was no longer in the presence of the voice, surrounded by light and love, I became intensely angry with my dog. I irrationally blamed Wuss for interrupting my heavenly experience and bringing me back to earth. I did not want to be back.

In addition to the anger was a new sense of fear. Now that I realized I was sprawled on my hard, dry lawn, I began to recall what I had been doing. Then the image of me being knocked unconscious (for the first time in my life ever, despite playing several full-contact sports as a teenager and a young man) flooded my mind.

I was seized with terror. Had I broken my back? Was I paralyzed?

I lifted my right hand slightly and moved my fingers. Then I spider-walked them to my pocket and found my cell phone. Thank goodness it had not gone flying too. Making sure to not move my body, I called Doug. He's an attorney in town, but in his earlier years, he had trained as an emergency medical technician. I also texted two friends who are physicians.

I don't know why, but I had an intense urge to get up. Not surprisingly, Doug ordered me not to move. He repeated that admonition. "Dad," he said, "you have all these doctor friends. Call them. You are not going to listen to me." But then he sighed. Doug knows me well; he knows my instinct is to push myself and not listen to others. So he instructed me on how to get myself up with the least potential damage, should I insist on doing so. I was to keep my head on the ground and my neck rigid as I brought my knees up. Then I was to roll slowly and gently over to one side, keeping my head in line with my spine. If there was no pain or other signs of injury, I could then reach my arms out and inch up to all fours, like Wuss (who was watching anxiously, wanting to play). Again, if I felt "normal," I could slowly stand, taking deep breaths and still holding my head and neck as still as possible.

After hanging up, I followed Doug's instructions and very slowly stood. My dog sniffed my feet and legs. I felt amazingly fine—just a little shaken with a sore knot on the back of my head.

Within minutes, several Houston Fire Department trucks and ambulances arrived. My physician friends had called 911 and directed the emergency crews to transport me to the medical center. The responders could not reach me, though. My backyard is completely bounded by a fence and a large steel gate. They began calling out questions as I walked over to them.

"Good afternoon," I replied. "I appreciate you coming, but I am just fine and won't be going anywhere," I said.

They stared for a moment, and then one, perhaps the crew leader, said something like, "Mr. Coleman, you've had a very bad fall and hit your head. You seriously could be suffering from head trauma and be in life-threatening danger. You really must be examined."

> *I did not want to go to the hospital. I felt just fine, miraculously fine.*

I continued to rebuff the advice. My cell phone buzzed as my friends kept calling or texting to convince me to get to the hospital. One told me to think of Natasha Richardson, wife of fellow actor Liam Neeson. She had struck her head while they were skiing and thought she was fine. That night she died of an epidural hematoma, a hemorrhage between the skull and the brain's covering, sometimes caused by a blow to the head—such as falling off a ladder.

Nevertheless, I refused. I did not want to go to the hospital. I felt just fine, miraculously fine. So after about thirty minutes, the emergency personnel gave up and left.

I went into the house. I fed Wuss. I warmed up some dinner and watched some television before going to bed. The next morning, a

Sunday, I awoke after sleeping soundly, with only that sore spot on the back of my head. I attributed it to a miraculous and divine intervention.

A Dramatic Personality Change

Nevertheless, later, after some reflection, I listened to one of my doctor friends and got myself checked out. I had no lightheadedness. My head did not hurt, and my balance felt typical. I wasn't drowsy. I could speak normally, and I wasn't confused. But I acknowledged to myself that there can be delayed symptoms after a concussion. I agreed to be treated with methylprednisolone, which fights inflammation.

There was indeed one symptom I eventually may or may not have exhibited. No one can tell me, and I don't know. Dramatic religious experiences like NDEs can lead to personality changes. So can head trauma. If I did suffer a temporal lobe brain injury, one of the side effects can be a certain degree of hypermania.

I became convinced that I had been spared by divine intervention in order to change my life.

Almost immediately after the fall and heavenly encounter, I underwent what I can only describe as an apparent spiritual transformation, wherein I became convinced that I had been spared by divine intervention in order to change my life and to influence those around me. I felt very close to God, and I only wanted to be closer.

On the Monday after the injury, I returned to my work as a mediator. My practice was one of the largest in the state of Texas. That day, I had two mediations scheduled, both of which ended successfully by resolution. I waived my fee. Something was different in the way I was feeling, and I couldn't put my finger on what it was.

I found myself emotionally tender. I felt the feelings of the people who brought disputes to me to mediate. Sometimes it would be almost overwhelming. I would cry in private several times daily, often about things that had been routine in my practice and life before the fall. This emotion was very unlike me.

By the middle of the week, I was becoming convinced that the successful resolution model, of which I had been a pioneer in starting and had used for twenty years, was flawed for lack of a spiritual element. Mediators are expected to be completely neutral and "stay in the question," showing no bias toward or involvement with either party in the conflict. Instead, I felt mediators should point out each side's strengths and weaknesses, including spiritual issues. I proceeded to do that.

Looking back, I can see my pronouncements probably sounded grandiose and overly spiritualized. They disturbed my clients. Because of long-standing relationships, many clients submitted to the new procedures. But I suspect they thought I was suffering from some kind of head injury that would heal, and things would revert to some normalcy. Some clients openly questioned my sanity, urging me to admit that my behavior was not rational. It would be a few months before I reached that stage.

Approximately five days after the fall and NDE, at the direction of a radiologist friend, I consented to undergo several CT scans and MRI scans. All results came back normal. I also underwent numerous blood tests, all also normal. I was even more convinced that I had not been injured in the fall and that my spiritual awakening was real.

However, I continued to show uncharacteristic behavior, giving away money and making rash decisions. In late November, I traded in my Mercedes for a new top-of-the-line pickup. I can't say why I did this.

Then I arranged to have it customized, with a carpeted camper shell and stereo system and many other features to an extent that was clearly "over the top." I had this delusion that I was going to load up my dog and we were going to go tour the world. Of course, I could not do that. I could not leave everything behind, including my children.

> *I could not sleep, sometimes for days. I was unable to quiet my mind. I was frightened and anxious.*

Next, I purchased, sight unseen, a house that had been the subject of a mediation I conducted—against the advice of a friend who is a real estate broker. The price did not seem extraordinarily high, but once I actually saw the house, I recognized that my decision was probably not a good one.

Nevertheless, I blazed ahead. I hired ten or so contractors to remodel and renovate it. By the end of November, I had given away or unnecessarily spent more than $150,000, on top of ordinary living expenses.

In my interpersonal relationships, I lost the patience to listen to others, believing instead that their issues were centered in an incorrect interpretation of God's universal truths. I was preachy with everyone, impatient that they should comply with my beliefs without question. When they did not, I would end the conversation. My mediation practice began to slow down.

I could not sleep, sometimes for three days and nights. I would lie in bed planning future events in my life and the lives of my children. I would toss and turn, sweating, unable to quiet my mind. I was frightened and anxious about whether I would be able to continue to meet my professional obligations and to function at the level that is expected of me. I was exhausted physically and emotionally. I lost more than sixty pounds in the first three months after the fall.

I began to research brain injuries. Although nothing was seen in my scans or lab tests, I began to suspect that I was exhibiting secondary mania following a traumatic brain injury. Yet, I knew God was with me. And I knew I was being nicer to people.

Then, after about three months, I awoke one morning feeling like the person I was before the fall.

I sold my truck and returned to driving the type of car I had driven for two decades. I rented out the house I had renovated at a very competitive rate. I regained my professional practice. And I ceased spending crazily and giving away my income, although I continued to tithe, donate to good causes like the Twenty-Four-Hour Club, and keep a small local church alive through financial support.

One change that did not fade was an intense interest in studying the Bible and all things related to religion. In the years since my near-death experience, my relationship with God has continued to grow deeper and deeper. He feels like a close friend. Getting close to Christ is undeniably the most important thing in my life.

Warts and All

Until a person experiences what I did, these are just words in a book. But they are not words to me.

Every time I try to describe what I saw and felt and learned, I feel a welling up of emotion inside. Teachings that I had heard all my life in church, concepts that I had *stopped* hearing because they just seemed abstract and dry, became living truths that now made eternal sense.

Before my NDE, I thought that God was continuously judging my behavior. Afterward, I realized that He loves me, warts and all. And everybody, not just me.

Although I am not seeking it, I am no longer afraid of death. I know that whatever awaits me in the hereafter, I will again be in the center of Christ's eternal and unconditional circle of love, wonderful beyond our wildest imagination.

My Life since My Near-Death Experience

Bryan Coleman

Before my near-death experience, my knowledge of God's love was shallow. Since then, my beliefs and spiritual practices have deepened.

Q How have you changed since your near-death experience?

A My spirituality is a priority in my life now. I attend church regularly and encourage my adult children to as well. I pray every morning, several times daily, and every evening before retiring. I try to read one or more Bible verses every day before I begin work, and I also try to read one or more daily devotionals. But these practices are not just for the sake of doing. Rather, I have a thirst for knowledge about God and have a complete awareness of Him in my life. These daily rituals allow me an opportunity to focus on God and the things He wants me to do in my life.

Q What kinds of things do you think God wants you to do?

A I am blessed to be financially stable due to my successful law practice. I completely support a small local church other than my own because it needs help and I think God wants me to do this. In addition to donating money to worthy causes, I also donate my time. During my NDE, I felt such love from God, and I realized I haven't always shown

His love to others. I do what I can now to share myself and my success with others and also openly profess my faith—and God's love—to others.

<hr/>

Q *How did your NDE change your relationships?*

A When I was growing up I knew my parents loved me. My mother was more open with her affection than my father. I, too, have had relationships with many people where I haven't been extravagant with expressing my love. This changed for me after my near-death experience, when I felt God's overwhelming love. Now my life is built around the first and second commandments: Love God with all your heart and love your neighbor as yourself.

My True Home

By Melinda Gross, as told to Hilarey Johnson

Let the words of my mouth and the meditation
of my heart be acceptable in your sight,
O LORD, my rock and my redeemer.

Psalm 19:14 (ESV)

I waited a long time to tell my story. I waited, because it was difficult to admit that I hadn't wanted to come back. My daughter was only one month old at the time, and I didn't want her to know how hard it was to leave a place of light, where I felt unconditionally loved, and return to incredible pain—even though I would be returning to her.

It was actually complications from her birth that led to that day.

I woke the morning of October 31,1990, having dreamed I was pregnant. My daughter was thirty-one days old, but I'd felt phantom baby kicks and movements in my dream that made it even more real. In fact, I was surprised when I woke up and discovered that I was not still pregnant.

As I rose and got ready for my day, I started to bleed. I did not have any bleeding problems prior to that day, so I called my doctor. He said flow can sometimes happen and not to worry, but to call back if it became very heavy.

I was happy for the doctor's answer because I didn't want to worry. My daughter and I had plans. We were going to see her father later that day.

My daughter's father used to be my boyfriend. When I initially told him about the pregnancy, he'd been very happy. But a few months later, he told me I should not keep the baby. He urged other solutions. He promised me we could have another baby together someday, that it just wasn't the right time. He pleaded for me to at least give up the baby, but I couldn't do that. With or without his help, or even my parents' help, I wanted to raise the child. You see, I had been adopted.

My Childhood Home

My adoptive family was very loving. I grew up with an older brother who was also adopted and a younger sister who was a biological child to our parents. We were all raised in the church, and my brother went on to become a minister. I was close to my parents and siblings, but I was very close with my adoptive grandfather. He was related to Sam Houston, an important leader of the Texas Revolution.

The family has amazing roots, but not just in building this nation. From them I learned what it meant to be a family, to share love, to be part of something. So while I knew that my baby could have a loving family if I put it up for adoption, I still wanted to keep it.

I grew up going to church every Sunday. From the very young age of four or five years old, I felt like I could see Jesus. I would search for Him in the clouds because I always felt like He was with me. At age fourteen,

I went through confirmation at my church, which required me to take vows that affirm my trust in Jesus.

I knew that for some people, church was simply a social activity; I felt like people only dressed up at church for social reasons. I didn't want faith to be like that for me. I wanted to know God, to learn about sacrifice and forgiveness, to continue searching for Jesus everywhere I looked. I turned to the Bible to try to get a better understanding, but it wasn't easy for me to read. In the end, I spoke very openly with my minister and he made the Bible palpable for me. He made me feel comfortable when I had theology questions like, "How do people on desert islands who've never heard the gospel learn about God?" He told me that was why we all needed to preach—to share God's message with others who might not have heard it by living my life through God.

> *For some, church was simply a social activity. I didn't want faith to be like that for me.*

But eight years later, in college, I became immersed in my ego. I planned to make lots of money with an engineering degree. I thought being strong and independent was the most important thing. I forgot about God.

Growing Up without God

I had also developed a serious relationship with a boy. I will call him Chris. We met when I was seventeen and a junior in high school. At the time he was twenty-two. I was so enamored with him, we even attended my senior prom. Both of my siblings married their high school sweethearts, and I assumed the same would be my path. Except, my parents didn't like Chris, in large part because of the significant age difference. It wasn't expressed, but I think my parents hoped the relationship would end when I graduated from high school. They would have preferred that I never saw Chris again when I left our hometown to attend Colorado State University in Fort Collins. But I did continue to see him.

In the beginning, I came home regularly to visit both Chris and my parents. At a certain point, though, my parents forbade me to see him. They must have realized that it was not a good relationship and may have started to see some of the signs of alcohol and physical abuse that I was yet to understand. Eventually, I started to come home to see Chris instead of them. One of the first times I came back to see only Chris was when the physical abuse began.

Chris hurt and scared me, and I spoke with a police officer after the incident. I didn't need to go to the hospital but I was naïve. I believed the incident was all my fault. I didn't understand that abuse typically follows a pattern. I never told my parents about what happened, or even that I had been in town. I didn't want them to know I was not honoring their wishes. I tried talking to Chris's parents, but they didn't believe me. I felt all alone.

Around the same time, I started to see glimmers of his addiction too. He drank—sometimes a lot. Occasionally, I wouldn't hear from him for days. It always seemed inexplicable. Sometimes he would get really angry seemingly for no reason; other times, he would be sweet and loving. He made so many promises to marry me during the five years we were together. Usually he would say, "Let's just go to the justice of peace, do whatever it takes."

Once, I believed his promise enough to put on a white dress and wait for him on top of Horsetooth Mountain with a friend at 11:00 a.m., the promised time. I found out later that he had been drinking heavily when he asked me to marry him during that instance. I see now that he was usually drinking when he promised marriage. I learned the hard way that he never kept the promises he made while he was inebriated. But still I didn't end the relationship.

> *I learned the hard way that he never kept the promises he made while he was inebriated.*

One day during those months of hope and disappointment, I discovered I was pregnant. Although I was still in college, I believed we would get married, raise our baby, and create a life together. It had been our plan to get married eventually anyway, I told myself. This just sped up the timeline. But my plan wasn't to be.

When I was six and a half months pregnant, Chris sat me down and said, "Listen, I cannot do this. I cannot be a father. I am an alcoholic." He detailed in a very sober way all of the blackout episodes, the DUIs, rehab visits and hospitalizations, and how his family had disowned him. I insisted that we stay together, that he owed it to me to take care of me, that I could take care of him too. Even though he didn't want any part of the responsibility of raising a child, he made me promise to not go on welfare.

After Chris shared all these details, I realized how long I had been in the dark. But even with all of that information as well as the threats, I still loved Chris and hoped we could be a family.

It was my third year studying chemical engineering at Colorado State University. My parents hadn't wanted me to be an unwed mother.

I went home for spring break and plopped down on the couch. My mom asked me what was wrong. "Nothing," I told her. But she knew me so well. She immediately asked if I was pregnant.

She was supportive when I assured her that Chris was supportive and that we would be married after I graduated. I told her that we had already planned to be married anyway, and in the meantime, he would come with me to doctor visits and contribute. Although Chris had told me he wanted nothing to do with the baby, I still believed he would help out and that we would eventually marry, which is why I told my mom what I did. My dad was not happy when I told him after he came home from work. He was pretty angry, actually, and needed to take a drive that night to cool off. My parents' greatest concern was that I would toss away all the time and money I had been dedicating to my education and not finish school.

> *My parents' greatest concern was that I would not finish school. Their fears weren't unfounded.*

Their fears weren't unfounded. As it was, I was struggling just to make average grades in college, whereas in high school, I had been a straight-A student. It was because of those high grades that a high school science teacher had encouraged me to pursue engineering.

But I was from a small town that didn't have a lot of resources. Most of my college peers who were pursuing an engineering degree had taken AP classes in high school. They didn't seem to struggle as much as I did no matter how many hours I spent studying or the amount of text I highlighted in my books. I couldn't pull a higher grade—even in my non-academic classes. I ran in the Boulder marathon, but I couldn't pass physical education.

My grandfather told me that I needed to put my schoolbook under my pillow so I could learn through osmosis. He teased me that I would absorb more information by sleeping on a book than I did when I exhausted myself looking at one. As with many other things, though, I didn't listen or ask for help. I was young, independent, and full of myself. I wanted to do everything on my own, in my way.

This included having a baby by myself.

Just Me and the Baby

My parents were present for the birth of my beautiful baby. Even my dad came around when he held his granddaughter. Chris did not come to the hospital, but after I got home, back to where I was living, he did come to visit us. When he met the baby, he was as in awe of her as I was. He came for a second visit, and then a third.

To my surprise and joy, during one visit he confessed that he had planted a pumpkin seed on the day our daughter was born. He said it was growing, and that he would bring me a pumpkin from the plant. I felt like my perseverance had been rewarded. It symbolically planted a seed of hope in my heart to know he was nurturing and watering something in honor of our daughter.

So when I woke that Halloween morning with heavy bleeding, all I wanted to think about was that when I saw him, our relationship might be fully restored. He may have only been seeking connection with his child, but I harbored hope for reconciliation as a whole family.

With the anticipation of his fourth visit I packed my backpack, bundled up my newborn in her carrier, and went to my heterogeneous catalytic reactor design class. I always sat in the front of the class with my nursing daughter on my lap. I'm sure we were an interesting sight to all of the other students in my class—all boys!

I was an unlikely candidate for engineering anyway, and not just because I was struggling with my grades. There were few females in the field at that time, and my brain didn't think in terms of equations, like most engineers. Instead, I had to sketch out my answers or write essays to learn.

Coming to the End of My Strength

After class that day, I took the bus across town to return home and get ready for Chris's visit. It was still morning, about 10:30, when the bus stopped at the busy intersection of Lemay and Mulberry. As the brakes squealed, I grabbed the rail to steady myself from the jarring motion of the bus.

The bus doors opened. With my daughter in my arms, I rose to unsteady feet and reached down to lift my backpack. A flutter deep inside my abdomen caught my attention. Before I could secure the backpack strap, I relived the phantom baby kicks that I'd had early that morning in my dream of being pregnant.

It felt off, though, different from the dream. I sensed something slipping away and then a warmness on my leg, under my sweats. I looked down to see blood between my feet. To my horror, a blood clot the size of a softball was lying on the floor of the bus.

I had to escape the crowd! I remember the stares of some other passengers, their eyes as wide as saucers. I don't think any of them had time to comprehend or understand what was happening as I uttered an apology, bent down, and picked up what I was able to of the blood clot.

The bus driver kept asking if I was okay—but I just wanted to flee my trail of blood.

I don't remember exactly what I was thinking, but I do remember feeling like a kindergartner who'd spilled her milk, who'd done something wrong. I rushed to get off the bus and away from everyone's shock.

I stumbled down the steps to the pavement. I was more aware of being appalled by what had come out of me in front of everyone than conscious of whether or not anyone offered me help. Looking back, I'm surprised I was still standing at that point. I was embarrassed for sure, but I was also so used to being on my own and taking care of myself that asking for help didn't even enter my mind.

I watched the cars zooming by on the three-lane highway. The sounds were deafening, and the gusts of wind pulled at me. I turned to hurry home, but in that moment, I understood I had an important decision to make. When I realized the hospital was closer to where I stood than my own home was, the decision became easy.

I pressed the button to cross the street and watched the red "Don't Walk" symbol as though it would change faster by my wanting. It seemed like an eternity passed while I waited for that crosswalk light to change to green. Then another eternity passed while I navigated my way in front of the stopped cars. I believe I was still bleeding, and I remember starting to feel dizzy. My singular focus became keeping my baby safe.

I remember starting to feel dizzy. My singular focus became keeping my baby safe.

When I got to the grassy lawn in front of the hospital, I could see several EMTs or other hospital workers just outside the emergency entrance. They were talking and leaning against the building, smoking cigarettes. I was faint but clear enough to know I wanted my daughter out of her carrier. I felt like I was going to collapse and didn't want to land on her. I waved at them, signaling with a bloody hand while trying to pull my baby loose with the other. I pulled her free just as we slumped to the cool grass together.

The next thing I remember is being in the emergency room. There, the doctors told me I was hemorrhaging—and that it was very rare thirty-one days after delivery. They thought the issue was probably a retained placenta and asked if they could put me under anesthesia and do a D&C, which would remove any remaining tissue.

After the procedure, as I was being moved into recovery, I began to gush blood again. Thinking they must not have gotten all the tissue, the doctors put me under anesthesia again and repeated the procedure.

When I awoke the second time, it was to agitated movement all around me. The hospital staff was trying to figure out how much blood I had lost and how much I was still losing.

As I lay in bed listening to them bustle around me, I began thinking strange thoughts. For instance, how the specific gravity of blood was similar to water, and how maybe the nurses could weigh my sheets to see how much I had lost. It seemed like a simple solution to me, but I didn't know how to convey it.

Soon, my thoughts began to turn to my daughter. I would need to breastfeed her before long. The nurses assured me they were taking good care of her. They had placed her in the maternity ward and she was taking a bottle. Then they told me they needed to do the procedure a third time and began to put me back under anesthesia.

Unfortunately, even that third D&C didn't stop the bleeding. The doctors decided to give me a drug that would clamp down my uterus. I didn't know if the drug was working on my uterus, but it felt like it was clamping down my heart and lungs. It was so painful.

The next thing I remember was the sun had set and I was being moved into the maternity ward so I could be near my daughter. The doctors told me that the drug had been a success—the bleeding had finally stopped.

Just after I was lifted from the gurney into the bed, I felt that same sensation I had felt on the bus, the one I described as something slipping away. I knew I must be hemorrhaging again but I didn't say anything. I was weak and tired, but I lay on the bed thinking that I could control the bleeding, make it stop, if I just focused on my breathing. Even after the three unsuccessful D&Cs and knowing I needed to get healthy in order to care for my daughter, I still didn't want to ask for help, to tell anyone what was happening. I believed I was invincible. I thought that I could breathe through what was happening and I would be fine. I was still so arrogant.

I believed I was invincible. I thought I could breathe through what was happening. I was so arrogant.

Later that night, the nurse came in and lifted my bedsheet. The atmosphere in the room quickly grew frenzied. I heard the code red being called and saw doctors running into my room. My limbs and then my whole body grew ice-cold. I knew I was going into shock. I heard someone say to call my parents, who lived 150 miles away.

One of the nurses put a blood pressure cuff on my leg because she couldn't get a reading from my arm. My heart felt like it was beating out of my chest. I knew I was bleeding out.

Someone else tried to start an IV for blood transfusions but couldn't get it inserted into either arm. So a nurse put an IV into my neck. He missed the first time and had to poke me in the neck twice to get the needle into my jugular. There wasn't time to warm the blood, and I remember feeling how cold it was as it flowed into my body. My heart rate was spiking. The same nurse who had been with me during delivery was with me now, only this time trying to get me to breathe.

> *In that moment I believed I was dying. I felt like a scuba diver at the bottom of the Atlantic and my air had just run out.*

Above all the loud voices, someone was calling out my dropping blood pressure: "Sixty over forty...forty over thirty...forty over twenty." The heart-rate monitor beeped, adding to the clamor of noise, but all I could focus on was the pain in every cell of my body.

In that moment I believed I was dying. I felt like a scuba diver at the bottom of the Atlantic and my air had just run out. I had no options. No hope of recovery. I was desperately afraid. It was then I realized I had no control. I was not as strong and capable as I thought I was.

And then I realized that I needed God's help. I wanted Him to rescue me in a different way than just knowing about Him from reading the Bible. I called out to Him in my thoughts. *God, please help me, please. I'm so sorry, God. I will follow You, God, until the end of my days. Just please help. I love You, God. Please help.*

On the Other Side

The pain was gone. In its place was supreme happiness.

I could still hear all the noise, and I remained lying on the bed in the busy room. But something shimmered in front of me. It was shaped like the privacy curtain a nurse draws around a hospital bed. This shimmering shape parted and lifted like a veil.

Suddenly, two beings were beside me. I somehow knew they were angels. One held my hand. I could both see our hands and feel the sensation of the angel's touch. The temperature of his hand was cooler than a human hand. His fingers seemed longer, and the texture of his hand and fingers was slightly smoother, like marble or glass. Other than that, the hand was the same as a human hand. It was very comforting.

In the distance behind the angels was a wide and gradually spiraling staircase that was backlit by an incredibly bright light. The light itself seemed to radiate joy, peace, and serenity. All those feelings enveloped me, shining out in the rays. The sounds of the chaotic hospital room were replaced by glorious harp music and singing. It seemed like the music was coming from the light. To me, it was like the light was a humming star that was singing to me.

The angels were bigger than humans, maybe eight feet tall. They were bent over in prayer kneeling next to my hospital bed. It felt enormously loving and supportive. I didn't see any wings on them. At first I thought this vision might all be a dream, but then the angels, the light, the music all felt completely natural, more "real" than life on earth. The one who held my hand told me that his name was Michael. He didn't speak out loud but rather into my mind. He had blue light emanating from him. His skin was perfect, and he had red lips; big, brilliant blue eyes; and black hair. He was wearing a blue tunic and looked similar to the statues of Michael the Archangel that I've seen in Renaissance paintings. The other angel was bathed in more of a golden light, and he wore a beige tunic. He, too, told me his name. I remember that it started with a C, but I don't remember what it was anymore. They both wore beige cloaks with hoods over their tunics.

> For a moment I did not realize that what I was seeing was actually me. My body was completely blue.

The next thing I knew, I had left my bed somehow and was moving toward the staircase, with the angels at my side. I must have been floating because I wasn't walking. I looked down to see my body below us. For a moment I did not realize that what I was seeing was actually me. My body was completely blue—not the skin itself, but the light surrounding it and coming from it.

Since Michael had spoken to me inside my mind, in the same way I asked him where he had come from. Michael said to me, "I have always been here. I am your guardian angel." I understood in that moment that both angels had always been with me.

We got closer to the staircase. It was extremely wide and looked as if it was made of marble. It had golden rails and a white runner. On the stairs behind the angels I saw several people I had previously known who were deceased. My uncle Harry and aunt Victoria were there, smiling at me. Uncle Harry was wearing one of his favorite flannel shirts, and my aunt Vic wore a lilac dress. They looked like younger versions of themselves. They seemed to me the way that they looked in older pictures.

I also saw our postman from when I was growing up. One other person I recognized was a young man who had been my brother's best friend in high school. He and my brother had planned to become college roommates before the boy drowned at age eighteen in Jackson Lake. He had been dead for four years at that moment. Fog, or a shroud of some sort, was around them. Farther in the background was still that bright light.

I was aware again of the hospital. Coming from one side I could hear the beautiful music and singing. On the other, I heard two women arguing. And I saw myself, still surrounded by blue light, but I could also see the EKG machine and other monitors. The EKG monitor showed I had flatlined. One of the people around me had defibrillator paddles, and a Roman Catholic priest was giving me last rites.

As this was happening, I flew past the fog, the postman, and the other people I saw. I felt as if I was being flown into space at the speed of light toward that bright light, the angels on either side of me. I realized that light was the total love of God. He and the light were the source of all love.

At the top of the stairs, I stood before an arch, similar to the kind of trellis you see in a garden. It was also smooth, white marble. It looked like it must have been about twelve feet high and twelve feet wide. It was covered in red, white, yellow, and pink roses. Beyond the arch were beams of light that I sensed were other beings, either angels or souls. And more roses—more than I could ever imagine. They were in shades more vibrant than I'd ever seen. All different colors. Their fragrance surrounded me, but it was sweet and beautiful, not overpowering. A beautiful expanse of grass was laid out between the arch and the beams, and a path cutting through it was edged with even more flowers.

Above the beams of light was a brilliantly blue sky. I felt warm all over, the kind of warmth I feel on a perfect day in July. In this comforting setting of sweet scents, warmth, and blue sky was a great and beautiful city.

> *I felt like I was flying, not walking, because I don't remember the sensation of my feet on the ground.*

The great city was off in the distance, appearing as if on a hill or in the clouds. Even though it seemed far away, I could see that the buildings were like white castles—sturdy and grand buildings that had windows without panes of glass.

My angels and I continued to move forward toward the city, but I felt like I was flying, not walking, because I don't remember the sensation of my feet on the ground. And then I was closer, and I knew I was at the gate of heaven. I felt unconditionally loved while surrounded by that bright light, and I had the specific feeling that I wanted to give as much love as I received. I also had the sense that we were all brothers and sisters, all one in God's love.

In the midst of this glory, I heard a voice. It boomed loud and deep, but as with the angels, only in my mind. I was told it was not my time. I knew this was God talking to me. I don't know how I knew that this energy of absolute, pure love was God, but I did.

I shouted, "But this is my true home!" I put up my best argument that this place where I was standing was where I belonged. I didn't want to leave this place of unconditional love!

I also knew it would hurt to return, and not just in the physical sense of the broken body I would return to. I knew the hurt would also come from leaving this place.

Then I heard my daughter crying. She was hungry. She needed me. I sensed then it was time to go, that my arguments wouldn't keep me there.

Off to the left there was another set of stairs leading downward. As I descended those stairs, away from the gate of heaven, pictures appeared in front of me, images recounting my whole life. I saw situations when I had been mean to people. These pictures weren't static, though. I could actually relive moments, like one when I was seven and threw a butter knife at my sister. But I relived it from her perspective. It was horrible, appalling even. Yet I also saw situations where I was kind to others, even small events like holding a door open for someone and letting a driver cut in front of me on the freeway. I realized that everything matters, that everything I did made a difference—good or bad—to someone else.

At that moment I looked down and saw myself on the hospital bed again. I was no longer blue. A doctor held my hand firmly in his; he looked sad. I wanted to comfort him, to cry out that I would be okay. I wanted to tell him that I was not in pain.

Next, I could see two nurses arguing in the hallway, the two voices I had heard before. One was being reprimanded for not checking on me for so long. I called out to them, "No, no, don't fight. It's okay. I'm all right. Please, don't fight." I don't think they heard me, though.

I had the sensation of flying through the hallway and seeing my daughter in the nursery. I realized how bonded I was to her in the month since she'd been born. I remembered holding her in the sunlight when she was jaundiced; how I had nursed her through her first ear infection. I loved her incredibly. She was a month old and looked so different, so mature next to the newborn babies.

Back to a Body of Pain

I woke in the ICU. It was morning and my parents were waiting by my bedside. They were smiling at me with broad grins and welcoming faces. I hadn't seen them since the day my daughter was born. They said, "You're back with us," and "So good to see you, honey." They told me that they loved me. They were such a welcome sight, and I felt so much happiness all around me. My mom said she would go get my daughter for me to hold.

But fear flickered in my mind. Would they be upset about the medical bills? I had no money to pay them. Would they want me to leave college and come home with the baby?

Almost instantly I felt at ease. That unconditional love I felt from God enveloped me again and allowed me to feel surrounded by the unconditional love that came from my parents. I'll never forget how they didn't even have worry lines on their foreheads. I kept searching their faces for them. They were so full of joy that it seemed to me like they were angels.

I felt exactly like Jimmy Stewart in *It's a Wonderful Life,* when he realizes the love of his family and town and wants to run through the streets shouting for joy. I tried to pull the tubes out of my arms so I could get up. I was ready to jump up from my bed and get started on midterms, on living life. I wanted to take that love I felt on the other side and share it with everyone. My parents urged me to lie still, but I simply said, "No. I'm alive. I've been given a second chance!"

My actual recovery was not easy. I got a secondary infection and was in the ICU for a week. The doctor was able to save my uterus with the hope that I could have more children, and I did eventually have another daughter. My parents were a great help to me in the recovery process. They took care of my baby and brought her back and forth to the hospital so I could feed her.

I never knew if my baby's father, Chris, had kept his promise to come see us on the day I bled out. We never reconnected during my recovery. I did see him a little while later, once. But I didn't try to make our relationship work like I had before I felt the true love of God.

> *I stopped thinking I was invincible. I knew that God had control of my life.*

After I was released from the hospital and felt well, I went back to school. I stopped trying to make things happen in my own power. I stopped thinking I was invincible. I knew that God had control of my life. I started to study smarter and ended up getting all As, just as I had in high school. I began to rest more and live my life with love first, not work.

My parents continued to help me with my daughter while I finished school. We still lived 150 miles away from each other, but we figured out how to make the distance issue work. Even though I was spending more time with my parents and renewing our relationship, I never told them what had happened when I was in the hospital. It wasn't until my mom got sick years later and went into hospice care that I ever mentioned heaven to her.

In the last moments of my mom's life I was able to encourage her to make the journey to heaven. I didn't want to tell her what had happened to me, but I wanted her to know that eternity waited for her. One of the nurses said, "You need to go in and tell your mom that it is okay to die."

So I went into my mom's room and held her hand. I told her she would be fine because angels would be there to help her. I told her it was okay to pass and that we would be okay as well. I could say it with confidence because I knew what was waiting for her.

Living a Life that Matters

I told you before that the reason I never shared my experience was because I felt guilty that I hadn't wanted to come back to my body of pain—and to my daughter. But one day in 2015, I listened to the *Coast to Coast* broadcast by Dr. Jeffrey Long. It was the first time I heard somebody put into the words the feeling of guilt I'd had about not wanting to return. I never wanted my child to know that given the choice, I would have abandoned her. Although I wasn't actually given a choice about coming back, I felt shame that I didn't want to return. With the help of Dr. Long and his understanding of the guilt that is shared by some NDE-ers, I realized that God's love transcends my shame, that He loves me unconditionally.

> *I realized that God's love transcends my shame, that He loves me unconditionally.*

Sharing God's love with others is how I live my life. I believe our whole life should revolve around what we can do for others; I believe that we are supposed to help each other at all times and in all situations. I don't make a lot of money, but God always provides for me, and that enables me to give to people who are in need. And I also recognize that God uses me to help people, including volunteering at hospice, the United Way, and the Red Cross.

Everywhere I go I want to convey that no matter what pain you are in, whether spiritual, emotional, or physical—no matter how deep the well you are in—you can cry out to God. He will hear and He will help.

We live in a world full of fear. Humanity tries to create distractions to alleviate the fear, but those only soothe temporarily. Since my near-death experience and conversation with God, I know that love conquers fear. I know that when I cry out to God, He hears me and helps me. And I know that we will die when God wants us to die, and that a beautiful eternal life with Him awaits.

My Life since My Near-Death Experience

Melinda Gross

It has been over thirty years since my NDE. Every experience in my life has brought me closer to God. Because of my near-death experience, I have realized the importance of talking to God daily, thanking Him and praying to Him. I am not afraid to reach out and talk to God. I know He talks to me too.

Q How did your NDE affect your relationship with Chris, your daughter's father?

A The experience made me realize that I am imperfect. Although I try to life my life through God, I know I make mistakes, but God still loves me.

It was my NDE that made me realize that Chris and I were cycling through a relationship of abuse. God helped me realize that I could still love Chris but that I could be free to leave him. And I did. I decided to let God love Chris unconditionally. In the end, Chris continued to make bad choices, and I think he was eventually incarcerated.

Q Did you share your near-death experience with your family, and if so, what was their reaction?

A I remained close with my parents while they were living and turned down jobs and further schooling in order to be near them. As I mentioned, I never told my mom about my NDE before she died, but I like to think that I eased her fear of dying and having an eternal life in heaven. I never mentioned my trip to heaven to my dad, either, but I had a conversation with him during which I offered the same assurance about eternity. He died unexpectedly but was able to tell the EMTs that he was ready to pass over. I wasn't there for my dad at the end, but I know I will see him again in heaven. His last text to me was that he had asked God to watch over me.

I raised my daughters in the same way I live my life—to be kind to others (humans and animals alike), to treat people with respect, to do what you can to help people. They are remarkable women and are an inspiration to me. When they got older, I told them about my NDE. They were surprised when I shared my experience but supportive and, I think, recognized that my conversation with God is what allowed me to create the life I have. They, too, are faithful women and trust God. My experience has removed their fear of death.

Q *What is the biggest takeaway from your NDE?*

A Being on the other side taught me that everything we do matters. Every little act, for good or bad, matters in this life.

Love Never Dies

By Linda Jacquin, as told to Stephanie Thompson

———— ◆ ————

But because of his great love for us, God,
who is rich in mercy, made us alive with
Christ even when we were dead in transgressions
—it is by grace you have been saved.

Ephesians 2:4–5 (NIV)

You might be surprised or think it unusual, but I've had not only one heavenly encounter during my seventy-four years but several. My first near-death experience occurred when I was four years old. My second was at age forty. Both involved my middle brother, Robert.

One could say I'm sort of an expert on near-death experiences. Besides having my own NDEs, I've been a member of the International Association for Near-Death Studies (IANDS) for three decades. Founded in 1981, IANDS is a nonprofit organization associated with the academic field for near-death studies. Its mission is to analyze and provide information on the phenomena of near-death experiences, as well as building a global understanding of these occurrences through research, education, and support.

I joined the IANDS board of directors in 1999 and served as vice president of the organization for six years. As their newsletter editor for another two years, I interviewed many other experiencers (those who come back from a near-death experience call themselves "experiencers") who unanimously reported that being allowed to return and resume their earthly life brings with it a profound responsibility. Many feel, as I do, that God has endowed them with a mission to share with others about what's waiting on the other side. By giving an eyewitness account, each of us spreads the message of God's overwhelming, unconditional love.

> *Many feel that God has endowed them with a mission to share with others what's waiting on the other side.*

Through our yearly IANDS retreats, I've listened to hundreds of other NDE-ers who've found comfort in knowing, as I do, that there is an existence beyond this life. Sharing together validates each of our unique experiences by reassuring us that we're not alone in this knowledge.

Some experiencers have had multiple NDEs. Why, you may ask? Of course, no one can know for sure (it's on my list of things I want to discuss with Jesus when I get to heaven and stay there), but one idea is that multiple NDEs are similar to a book series. Each NDE builds and expands on the other. It's a continuation of knowledge for the experiencer—knowledge for us to use in our personal lives and knowledge to share with others during this lifetime.

Another hypothesis is that once the portal between realities has been opened, the soul finds its way between worlds more easily. Researchers indicate that most of us NDE folks are acutely aware of other forms of spiritual activity. We've had visions, been visited by beings from a heavenly realm, and some of us have seen angels.

Almost all experiencers I've talked to possess an urgency and readiness to be led by the spirit of God to share their NDEs with believers and non-believers alike. The overpowering love and compassion they received while in another realm gives them a deep desire to tell others what lies ahead.

The world is broken and hurting. People are questioning God and His purposes. They wonder what life is all about and if death is the end. We experiencers don't have all the answers, but we can give testimony of what happened to us. Most of us feel a pressing responsibility to reassure those who are searching that heaven really does exist. This life isn't the end of our existence. God and eternity are real.

With love as my compass and compassion my guide, I wish to share my experience with you. Here is my heavenly encounter. I hope reading my story blesses you.

Emotional Pain

That week in September 1988 had been horrible. I found out that my brother Bob had died over the weekend while spending time at the lake with his coworkers. I couldn't believe it. Bob was still a young man—only forty-seven years old.

His group was on the water at Kentucky Lake. Bob had just finished his turn skiing behind the boat. He let go of the rope, swam to the ladder, and climbed over the side. Suddenly, he raised his hands and clutched his head. His body went limp. He collapsed on the deck. Coworkers desperately tried to revive him, but Bob died instantly. In a blink, he was gone.

His wife, Joann, called me, crying. She said the coroner suspected a brain aneurysm. I was beside myself with grief. We all were. The middle of my three brothers, Bob was seven years older than me. Gentle, kind, and thoughtful, he never teased or picked on me like some older brothers did—like Ken, one of my other brothers who was four years older.

Bob and I had a special connection. A bond. I had always been partial to him. Now that he was gone, I worried. *Did he know how much I loved him?* I didn't get to say goodbye or to tell him how special he was to me. I never looked him in the face and said, "I love you, Bob." Now, it was too late.

A Love of Family

I grew up in a big Catholic family in Cape Girardeau, Missouri, with my siblings, Jan, Ray, Marilyn, Bob, Ken, and Sharon. I never met my sister Marilyn because she died when she was eleven months and eight days old. Even though her life was short, Mom always included her and made sure we kids remembered her too. Like many families, everyone pitched in. We all had chores, and the older kids were often called on to watch the younger ones.

Our father also did his share of household duties, in addition to his job at the Florsheim shoe factory. He left early for work, before we kids were awake, but he was home by three o'clock when we got home from school.

Daddy was a great cook. He prepared many of our meals. That was a big help because Mom worked for Southwestern Bell as a telephone operator. She was able to work split shifts so she could work while we kids were at school or asleep and then come home to care for our family too.

After Mom had Sharon, Daddy's mom, Grandma Reiker, came to live with us. Sharon and I were only twenty-two months apart. My parents needed an extra hand, or maybe an extra set of arms, to get the household chores accomplished while still nurturing and providing lots of attention to Sharon and me.

That's where Grandma came in. Mom used to say that Grandma loved to sit in the big wooden rocker with me.

"She would just rock, and rock, and rock you girls," Mom said, with a laugh on many occasions as she retold the story. "Grandma wanted to hold you all the time. We thought she rocked you so much that you'd surely have brain damage."

Of course, that was Mom's way of letting me know how much my grandmother loved me. Even though Grandma died when I was a toddler, I remember the affectionate feelings we shared.

> *Even though Grandma died when I was a toddler, I remember the affection we shared.*

A Special Relationship

I adored my family and all my siblings, especially my brother Bob. Protective and loving, he was the perfect guardian who was always looking out for Sharon and me, his little sisters. He made sure I always did the right thing.

"You're gonna get in trouble if you don't do what you're s'posed to," warned Bobby.

He often helped me with my chores and admonished me to behave when I didn't want to do as my parents instructed. To hear my family tell stories about my childhood, I was an independent girl—and maybe a little stubborn at times too. I never understood why, but Bob and I had a special bond.

As we got older, life took over. I couldn't remember the last time we'd sat and talked. Years before mobile phones, long-distance rates weren't cheap. Our phone calls were mainly a means to relay information.

About the only time Bob and I got together was when my family drove to Cape Girardeau to see my parents for holidays. The hustle and bustle of many people in a house didn't lend itself to deep conversations.

> *My faith taught me that one day we'd be reunited.*

Like many middle-aged folks, we were busy with families and jobs. I'd started my own advertising and promotion business four years earlier. Anyone who knows about being self-employed understands you put in many more hours than you do when working for someone else. Even though I had the luxury of working from home, I kept a strict schedule. I saw clients and made phone calls until the kids came home from school. Many times I'd slip away and continue to work once everyone in the house had gone to bed.

Bob was busy too. Married, he had two daughters and worked long hours. The responsibilities of daily life consumed us.

And now he was gone. *Why didn't I make the two-hour drive from my home in Wentzville, Missouri, to visit him in Cape Girardeau more often?* Now, I'd never see or hear from him again, at least not this side of heaven.

I loved him dearly. Days after his death, I missed his tender spirit already. *Did he know how much I loved him? Did he know how much I cared?*

I was beside myself with grief. Thankfully, Bob was a believer. My faith taught me that one day we'd be reunited. I knew God had a plan, but since I still had three children at home, I wasn't eager to leave them just yet.

Still, I couldn't shake my sadness. The only comfort I had was that Bob was now with our beloved Grandma Reiker in heaven. Two of my favorite people, whom I'd loved dearly, were now together for eternity, but knowing that didn't lessen my emotional pain.

Days later, our family—my husband, three children, and me—drove to Cape Girardeau from our home in Missouri for Bob's funeral. His widow, his two teenage daughters, my siblings, and my parents all dressed in black was the saddest sight I'd ever seen. We mourned greatly as Bob's coworkers and many people from the church and community we'd grown up in gave us their condolences. After the service, we all went back to Mom's house. We talked about the good times in the past and cried about a future without Bob and his abiding love and devotion.

Physical Pain

Ten days after Bob died, I found myself doubled over in pain. I awakened in the wee hours of the morning, my body in the fetal position beneath the covers of our bed. My stomach ached so badly—a severe, stabbing pang in the upper right side of my abdomen.

"Gerald," I groaned to my husband. "Something is wrong with me. My stomach really hurts."

He offered to get me an antacid and aspirin. I even tried a hot water bottle. But nothing helped.

I'd struggled with polycystic ovarian disease. After my youngest child was born a decade before, I had a hysterectomy and an oophorectomy, an operation to remove my ovaries. I was no stranger to internal abdominal problems, but this was a different sort of pain. A feeling like I'd never experienced before. Excruciating. I didn't know what was going on, but the intense pain lingered for hours. I couldn't go back to sleep. I couldn't get comfortable. The situation became unbearable.

"You've got to go to the emergency room," Gerald urged, as he punched in the emergency numbers and called an ambulance.

He helped me put on my robe. When the EMTs arrived, he brought them into the bedroom. He came with me while our three children, ages ten to seventeen, stayed behind to get ready to go to school.

I prayed, asking God to send angels to protect and watch over me.

The sun peeked above the horizon as the crew loaded me into the back of the ambulance and rushed me to the Wentzville Community Hospital, about five miles away.

In the emergency room, the doctor pulled back the curtain partition of the examination cubicle. I lay on the gurney on my side, hugging my knees to my chest. After a brief examination, he called a specialist to take a look. They admitted me to a hospital room. A young nurse brought a warm blanket.

"Fresh from the dryer," she said with a smile. "This will help you feel better."

The cozy covering and the nurse's considerate act comforted me. I was given medication to ease the pain. Technicians and nurses came in and out of the room, checking my vital signs, drawing blood, taking X-rays and abdominal ultrasounds, and administering other tests. Finally, I had a diagnosis. There was a serious obstruction and life-threatening blockage in my pancreatic and bile ducts. I would need immediate surgery. I spent the night in a hospital bed. The operation was scheduled for the following day.

I asked Gerald to contact our family and friends to pray for me. I also prayed for myself, asking God to send angels to protect and watch over me. Although I was a believer, Gerald and I didn't have a church home in Wentzville. We'd fallen away from organized religion. Sadly, I'd fallen away from God too.

A Youth of Faith

I used to have a deep faith. Raised in the Catholic church, I attended Mass with my family every Sunday at St. Mary's Catholic Church. My siblings and I went to the adjoining St. Mary's School through eighth grade. I continued my Catholic education and graduated from Notre Dame High School in 1966.

Our church and school were less than a block away from our house. We kids beat a path going there six days a week. Cutting through the alley behind our backyard, we were there in a matter of minutes.

A lifelong Catholic, I recited the prayers and knew the church history, but some of my fondest memories came from sitting in the pew. I remember being captivated by sunbeams that shone through the stained-glass windows. Minuscule dust particles floated through the air. They glittered and sparkled. Their glow gave me a familiar feeling of comfort that I could never explain.

As a grade-schooler, I remembered looking at the white statues of Jesus on the Stations of the Cross and thinking, *Why aren't You talking to me?* Somehow, I knew the depiction of Christ was wrong, that Jesus didn't look like the cold plaster renderings I saw in the church building. How someone as young as I was would have that understanding, I'll never know.

Religion was talked about a lot at home too. My parents had a crucifix on their bedroom wall. I solemnly considered Christ, who gave up His life for me, each time I passed it. But my favorite depiction was the long-haired Jesus with a pleasant face and eyes that peered deep into my soul. I'd seen Him in the pages of my prayer book. The picture of Him dressed in a robe of white, ascending into heaven after His crucifixion, was a favorite. God's plan of love and redemption had prevailed.

> *When I was contemplative, I realized I missed my spirituality. I yearned to be near God again.*

But now the religion of my youth didn't seem to fit anymore. I rarely talked to God unless there was a problem or I needed something. When I was contemplative, I realized I missed my spirituality. I yearned to be near God again, but I never did anything to rekindle that relationship.

Surgery Scheduled

Gerald sat in a recliner next to my hospital bed most of the day and then went home to stay overnight with the children. Even though the blockage was serious, I believed I was in good hands with the doctors. Still, the thought that I might go before my time, as Bob had, only days before, taunted me.

The next morning, a technician wheeled me down the hall to the surgical suite. I relaxed and felt woozy as the painkillers kicked in. I must have fallen asleep before we made it into the operating room.

A few hours after my surgery, I awakened groggily in the ICU. The rhythmic beeping of the heart monitor's cadence reminded me of my alarm clock's annoying buzz when it needed to be snoozed. I opened my eyes slowly. Several wires and tubes were attached to my body. A couple monitors and an IV pole crowded my bed.

"Is it over?" I mumbled to the nurse who stood at my bedside.

Her eyes radiated concern. "How are you feeling?" She bent close to my face.

"I...I...don't know," I said, but truth be told, I was exhausted. I felt as if I'd run a marathon. Physically, mentally, and emotionally, I was spent.

The doctor entered the room. He stood by the nurse's side.

"You had a grand mal seizure on the operating table," he said, putting his hand on my shoulder. "You're gravely ill. We've called your family."

He explained that the medication I'd received for the procedure had caused a reaction. I'd had a dangerous seizure during surgery.

I wanted to ask the doctor more questions about the seizure, procedure, and my prognosis, but I was incredibly sleepy. I'm not sure if it was the lingering effects of the anesthesia or if having a seizure made me feel so lethargic. All I wanted was to rest. In any case, I couldn't force my eyelids to stay open. Everything faded to black, and I could no longer hear the incessant beeping of the ever-present audio wallpaper that monitored my heartbeat.

A Visit from Bob

In the next moment, a bright white light shone around me. As piercing as the light was, oddly it didn't hurt my eyes. Not only did I see the brilliant illumination, but I felt it too. In fact, this stark light felt extremely comforting, like the cozy, soft blanket the kind nurse gave me when I checked into the hospital the day before. But this warmth covered me deep into my spirit.

> *I didn't know for certain where I was, but somehow I understood that I'd entered another realm.*

Its radiance enveloped me in an overwhelming feeling of love. As a result, emotions of affection bubbled up from inside of me. I sensed this light was good, pure, and holy, the essence of unconditional love. It was like nothing I'd ever seen or felt before, yet at the same time, it was familiar. Still, I was certain I'd never before seen any dazzling light that was similar to this one.

I realized I was no longer in the hospital, lying in an ICU bed and hooked up to an array of machines. I didn't know for certain where I was, but somehow I understood that I'd entered another realm. A heavenly realm, but I wasn't in heaven. Not yet.

In front of me, also in that light, appeared my brother Bob. The vibrant glow that surrounded him was peaceful and comforting. The same bright white light illuminated his face, and his blue eyes were effervescent like sapphires. They were as clear as a freshwater stream. His black hair fell softly across his forehead. This image of Bob reminded me of the brother I knew when he was a boy, maybe eleven or twelve. Same kind eyes. Same gentle spirit. It was as if I could see and feel his considerate, compassionate soul as I looked at his face—this solitary image of his face that gazed back at me.

Bob's tender expression exuded the love he had for me—the love that still existed even though he had departed. I felt his care, his protection. His essence swirled around me and ran through me. I was overwhelmed with feelings of adoration as Bob's love for me mixed with the love that was in this place.

Suddenly, I remembered Bob had died. A longing came over me.

"Are you okay?" I asked with urgency. "Are you happy?"

It was as if I could read his thoughts. Bob's face moved close to mine. So close that I could reach out and touch him, but I didn't. I intuitively knew he was safe here in this place. I understood Bob was happy, comforted, and unafraid.

I sensed he had something to tell me. Something important.

"Linda," he said patiently, in his older-brother way. It was as if he were still with me, teaching me, guiding me like he had all of his life. He spoke to me—not aloud with his voice, but through my thoughts. "It is not your time. You cannot stay. You have to go back."

As always, Bob was telling me the right thing to do. But I felt so much pain in my body that I resisted. I wanted to stay here, pain free, basking in his love. I really wanted to go with him. He looked radiant. And the love in that place was irresistible. It captivated me.

Bob said again, "Linda, it is not your time."

At that moment, I understood he was right. I remembered my three children—Jeremy, Tara, and Ashley. My husband, Gerald. I knew they still needed me.

As I drew in a deep breath, Bob's peaceful face faded far, far away from me. The light surrounding him grew dim until it was no more.

Recovering and Discovering

The *beep, beep, beep* of the ICU heart monitor returned. I opened my eyes. A different nurse, one I had never seen before, stood by my bedside. She looked to be about my age, wore a white uniform, and had the most compassionate expression on her face.

"I just saw my brother Bob," I exclaimed, weakly raising my head off the pillow. "He died last week."

Even though I was still feeling a little confused and dazed after the surgery, the experience with Bob was crystal clear, sharp, and vivid. I knew it was real. It wasn't a dream.

"It's okay," she said, patting my hand. Her eyes locked on to mine. Her voice was calm, reassuring. "You've had a near-death experience."

Near-death experience? What was that? Even though I'd never heard the term and had no idea what a near-death experience was, I felt comforted by her acknowledgment. In my mind I understood the nurse was validating what had happened to me. She affirmed the event was real. But before I could ask any questions of her, I nodded off to sleep.

When Gerald arrived at my bedside, concern knitted his brow. He'd spoken to the doctor. The physician came in and explained the bandage covering my abdomen had limited my lung capacity. A pulmonologist was called in and discovered I'd developed double pneumonia within the last twenty-four hours. Uncommon, but not unheard of, according to the medical staff.

After a couple of days on antibiotics and intravenous fluids, I was well enough to be transferred out of ICU into a step-down unit at the hospital. Healing was a process. I worked with physical therapists to get my strength back. I'd gotten so weak that I couldn't walk.

I stayed in the hospital a little over a week, but I never saw that mysterious nurse again. I caught myself wondering if she was real, but of course I knew she had to be. She talked about a near-death experience—something I'd never heard of before, so I couldn't have made that up in my mind.

In the weeks after my recovery, her face and her words faded from my mind. I focused on getting well and resuming my busy life. While I forgot about the nurse, I did recall seeing Bob in that otherworldly place. His insistence that I had to go back perplexed me. *Go back to where?* Was it a dream? A vision? I had no idea.

Recuperating and Remembering

The doctor said I would have a long and arduous recuperation. He was right. It took me at least six months to regain my strength. And as my body was getting back to normal, something out of the ordinary started happening.

One evening when I was running water in the tub for my bath, an image flashed before my eyes. I saw strands of golden blond hair, about eight inches long, floating on top of flowing dark water. In a blink, the picture disappeared. *What did it mean?*

> *I recall seeing Bob in that otherworldly place. Was it a dream? A vision? I had no idea.*

Every so often, the odd scene flashed in my mind. It came to me again and again. Strands of blond hair floating on top of the water in a river or stream. Nothing more. *Was it a recurring memory? A vision?*

These episodes occurred at random times. Sometimes I saw the mental picture when I was doing everyday chores. Other times, the scene infiltrated my thoughts when I was relaxed and not thinking about anything in particular. It was like a bookmark in my brain. I didn't know if it was a personal memory or a reminder of something I'd once seen on television or in a movie.

I didn't know who to talk to. Gerald and I had been married for two decades, but he wasn't an introspective or spiritual person. I didn't think he'd understand. I wondered if anyone would understand the bizarre occurrences I'd been having. *Was I losing my mind?* I worried that anyone I talked to would think I was crazy. The only person I could confide in at this point was God.

Perhaps this strange vision was also from the spiritual realm and I just couldn't remember it the way I could seeing Bob. *Please show me what it means.* I prayed for clarity, over and over, and took my questions and unanswered prayers to the only One I felt could understand.

A Divine Appointment

Wentzville was a small town west of St. Louis, and we'd lived there for several decades. Because of my advertising and promotion sales company, as well as my outgoing personality, I knew a lot of people. Chamber of commerce, civic clubs, and the kids' school activities provided me with an extensive network. I even knew about the people I didn't know—like my chiropractor's husband. I'd heard he was a counselor, but I'd also heard he was a regressive hypnotherapist. As fate, or God, would have it, he was at his wife's chiropractic office one day after my appointment.

I saw him at the front desk as I was checking out. I introduced myself and screwed up my courage.

"Jim," I stammered, a little embarrassed, "I want to ask you a question. I wonder if you could help me with something."

Jim smiled. "I'll sure try."

I lowered my voice. "I've been having a recurring vision—or maybe it's a memory. Something I don't understand. I wondered if I could talk to you about it sometime."

His compassionate eyes glowed with understanding.

Whatever this vision was, I needed to find out about it. I yearned to make sense of the image in my mind.

"Of course, Linda," he answered. He reached into his pocket and pulled out a business card. "Call me anytime."

I inhaled deeply and smiled.

That next day, I made a morning appointment for the week after next. I wanted to see him when the kids were at school and my schedule was open. I didn't want to feel pressured or distracted. Whatever this vision was, I wanted—no, I *needed*—to find out about it. It was like a puzzle with missing pieces, and I yearned to make sense of this image in my mind—to put it together and see the whole picture. I had to know what was happening and why I kept seeing the blond hair in the water.

Jim and I met in the small consultation room at his wife's chiropractic office. We sat in comfy chairs across from each other and made small talk. He instantly put me at ease. His manner was peaceful. I relaxed and trusted him. I felt very safe.

"Do you want to talk about what you've been seeing?" he asked.

I closed my eyes. The image appeared.

"Blond hair floating on water," I whispered. I felt as vulnerable as a child, yet at the same time, I felt Jim was a secure confidant.

Jim was quiet for a moment. "It's time to remember what that's all about," he said softly.

I sat in the chair and waited. Within a few moments, that day unfolded before me.

A Childhood NDE

That summer afternoon, our family was at a picnic. Mom sat on a big patchwork quilt under a massive oak tree. Our family's feast was in assorted containers. Other people were there too. I recognized the faces of friends from church. It looked like we'd just finished eating.

Mom's best friend, Bernadine, and her toddler daughter joined us on the blanket. My two-year-old sister, Sharon, and Bernadine's daughter laid down for a nap.

It was time for my nap, too, but I didn't want to go to sleep. I saw the other kids splashing in the water. They ran and laughed as they played near the shore of the creek. Now four and a half, I begged Mom to let me go and play by the bank too. I'd brought my new pail and shovel. I was so proud of them, and I couldn't wait to start digging in the dirt.

Mom agreed on one condition.

"Bobby, I want you to watch Linda," she hollered. Bob, my beloved middle brother, was eleven. He stood with a group of his friends by some trees by the shore.

He nodded and walked toward the quilt. "Yes ma'am."

Bobby held out his hands to me. I grabbed my red bucket and matching shovel and ran to him. He bent over and scooped me up. I gripped his waist with my thighs as he carried me on his hip. Together, we went to play near the shore.

I had a wonderful time digging in the dirt. After a while, I took off my shoes so I could wade in the water. It was easier to dig in the wet ground.

I pushed my shovel into the sandy shore and uncovered pebbles. *Plink. Plink. Plink.* I liked the sound they made as I dropped them into the tin bucket. I pushed a strand of my shoulder-length blond hair behind my ear so I could see all the shiny stones that glimmered at me from the bottom of the creek.

In Too Deep

As I stepped forward and reached for another pebble, the water that had been shin high rose to my chest. There had either been a drop-off or I stepped in a hole. In any case, the current ran fast. It swept my feet out from under me. I panicked because my toes couldn't touch the bottom. All of a sudden, my willowy frame was carried downstream.

I panicked. My toes couldn't touch the bottom. All of a sudden, I was carried downstream.

The water rose to my chin. It splashed my face. My eyes burned. I was just a little thing and didn't know how to swim. I couldn't fight the undertow. It happened so fast. I didn't know what to do.

The force pulled me toward a hollowed-out ledge that protruded from the bank. A large tree trunk with a tangle of branches and roots made a sort of overhang, a catchall for debris that floated in the current.

The water was deep there. I gulped mouthfuls of the creek water as I tried to keep my head above it. My foot caught on something below. Terror gripped me, and my head went under.

I was floating in the air above the creek. I saw myself in the dark, murky water.

At that moment when my body was submerged, my spirit popped up out of my body. I was floating in the air about twelve feet above the creek. I saw myself in the dark, murky water, my blond hair floating just beneath the surface.

Fear surged through me. I felt like I was going to cry, but my tears never came. I was horrified seeing the image of myself in the creek. I didn't know what to do. I was just too little to make those types of decisions on my own. Usually Mom or Bobby was around to guide me.

Drifting Away

I began to drift higher in the sky, farther away from the creek, the picnic, and my golden hair floating on the water. I didn't know what to think or feel. I didn't understand what was going on.

Around me everything was now white and bright. I looked to my right and saw two men. I thought they might be brothers. They were dressed in white flowing robes. I somehow knew they were angels. They didn't have wings, but they were next to me in the bright, white light. I intuitively understood they were celestial beings.

I had a sense that they were different ages, one older and one younger. The younger angel saw I was confused and quickly grabbed me up in his arms. He held me on his hip like Bobby did.

"She needs to go back," said the one who was holding me. I heard his words audibly; his tone was concerned.

Before I could say anything, the older angel patiently spoke to the younger angel, like a teacher might.

"It is her choice."

I felt bewildered. I didn't know what was going on. Dazed, I tried to figure it out.

The angels must have understood my confusion. At that moment Grandma Reiker, my father's mother who had died earlier that year, appeared. I saw her at a distance at first, then in the time it takes to snap one's fingers, she swooshed in close to me.

Grandma stood in front of the angels. She held out her arms. The angel who held me on his hip gently handed me to her. With that, they vanished. It was just Grandma and me. In Grandma's arms, I instantly felt safe. She cradled me close, my head beneath her neck. The uncertainty I'd felt earlier evaporated. I was safe and loved in the arms of my grandma.

I looked around. The atmosphere around us was filled with sparkles. The shimmering sparks reminded me of a pure clear icicle when light refracts off of it. I was captivated by the vibrant colors as they glowed in the space that surrounded me. As brilliant as the Fourth of July fireworks against the velvety black backdrop of the night sky, these colorful sparks illuminated the pale atmosphere that surrounded us. They made everything come alive.

Then Grandma spoke in my mind.

"Linda, if you go back, you will learn many things," she said encouragingly, in her sweet elderly voice.

> *I understood that a divine presence had joined us. I turned my head and saw Jesus.*

But I loved Grandma. I wanted to stay with her now more than ever.

"I don't want to," I replied firmly.

I wasn't upset, but I'd made up my mind. I was told that even at four and a half, I could be outspoken and maybe a little stubborn.

Grandma turned her face toward mine and looked down at me. As she did, I was filled with awe. I was enveloped with a remarkable feeling and intuitively understood that a divine presence had joined us. I felt a hand on my shoulder.

I turned my head and saw another familiar face—Jesus. Not the crucified Christ from my parents' bedroom, but the long-haired brunette Jesus that smiled at me from the pages of my children's prayer book.

He wore a long robe like the priest at church wore on Sundays, only Jesus's robe was pure white and seemed to glow.

Like the angels before her, Grandma handed me over to Jesus, then slowly faded out of sight. Jesus cradled me in His arms. I looked up and saw His beautiful face. His gaze burrowed deep into my soul. Pure love enveloped me. I felt safe.

As Jesus held me in His arms, He repeated what Grandma had said.

"If you go back, you will learn many things," He said tenderly.

But I wanted to stay. I felt safe. The love in this place fascinated me. I wanted to stay now and for eternity. I knew I was home.

The Panic Below

Just then, the atmosphere below me opened up. I looked down and saw a panoramic view of the shoreline. People were running around. But instead of laughing and playing as they had been earlier, everyone was frantic and panicked. Some ladies were weeping. People had shocked and horrified expressions on their faces.

Somehow I could read their thoughts. In my mind I heard what they were thinking. The people were desperate, terrified. And it was because of me.

Then I saw Bobby.

He looked scared. Ashen faced. Tearstained cheeks. I felt his emotions. Bobby was sad. So very sad. He blamed himself.

I could hear a thought that was running through his mind. It was Mom's voice: *Bobby, you keep an eye on Linda.*

Bobby was making himself feel so bad with that thought. He believed it was his fault that the current pulled me down into the water. I felt all of his hurt, grief, sadness, and shame. It broke my young heart.

I couldn't let Bobby feel like that! I didn't want him to shoulder the burden of my death. I knew what I had to do.

The Decision to Return

I gotta go back," I exclaimed to Jesus in a loud voice. "I gotta go back for Bobby! Bobby's gonna to be in a lot of trouble if I don't go back!"

And with that, Jesus was gone. I floated in that realm all by myself, but I was no longer confused or afraid.

I continued to watch the action on earth unfold. A man carried my limp body out of the water. Those beautiful, iridescent sparkles of light I'd seen in this place now decorated the space between where I watched from above and the horrific scene that was playing out down on the shore. The sparkles whirled above the heads of the people. Tiny, sparkling orbs, very much like the sunbeams I'd seen through the stained-glass windows at church, floated up from the earth.

> *I realized the twinkling sparkles were prayers from people pleading that I wouldn't die.*

I realized then what these twinkling sparkles were. They were prayers. Prayers for me. People were pleading that I wouldn't die. They begged for me to be okay. Their whispered requests swirled together into a beautiful melody. They prayed in one accord, yet the words of their individual prayers danced around to form an orchestra of petitions pleading for my life. Their song was full of love and life, with lyrics that were heartfelt requests I wouldn't die. The prayers of these people came from deep inside their hearts and souls, a desperate symphony of pure, unselfish love.

I noticed Bobby again. He stood away from the crowd and away from the man who brought me out of the water onto the shore. Physically and emotionally, Bobby was alone. I sensed that he would never be the same if I stayed.

His despondence was too much for me to bear. I wanted more than anything to be back in my body. As much as I loved this heavenly realm, Grandma, and Jesus, I wanted to help Bobby. And to do that, I needed to be alive again.

The man laid me down on the ground. He hovered over me. He pushed on my chest and breathed into my mouth.

At that moment, my spirit instantaneously zoomed back into my physical body. Lying there on the ground didn't feel good at all. I had horrible pain on my insides. I sucked in quick breaths as I coughed up creek water. My eyelids fluttered. I started crying.

Bobby rushed toward the crowd—toward me as fast as he could. He hit the dirt and crawled through the legs of the people who stood around me.

"Linda!" he cried. "You're okay!"

Finally Processing the Amazing Experience

Jim sat across from me and listened as I recounted the event. When I finished, he asked, "How do you feel?"

I drew in a deep breath. "Amazed and awestruck," I said slowly, "but also satisfied. It's like the pieces have all come together and I can see the completed puzzle, but I can't believe it all really happened to me. How could I not recall such a monumental occurrence as this until now?"

Jim raised his eyebrows. "That's a good question," he said, then chuckled. "Sometimes answers bring more questions."

I sat in silence for a moment and thought about the two parts of my story—what physically happened at the creek that day and what spiritually took place when my soul left my body.

"How do I know what I remembered is real—that I was truly in a heavenly place?"

Jim thought for a moment. "I wonder if you could talk to a family member who was there. If the details of what happened that day at the creek match up, it would validate your memory."

I figured I could find someone to confirm the events at the creek, but I didn't know if anyone could verify my out-of-body experience. After all, that only happened to me.

"Can people really leave their bodies?"

Jim leaned forward in his chair. "We don't know a lot about out-of-body experiences, but research has been going on for a few decades. It's a phenomenon in which a person perceives the world from a location outside their physical body."

I nodded my head. I remembered watching the events from above. If I could confirm the creek incident, I'd have no reason to doubt what spiritually happened to me either.

> "When your physical body was drowning in the creek, your soul separated and had an otherworldly experience."

"You also seem to have had a near-death experience. When your physical body was drowning in the creek, your soul separated and had an otherworldly experience, a heavenly encounter, if you will, when you were in another realm."

A near-death experience. At that moment, I remembered the mysterious nurse when I awakened in the ICU months ago. She mentioned a near-death experience. I told Jim about her. I also recounted how I saw my brother Bob when I went into an all-illuminating white light.

"Maybe you've had two NDEs," Jim said. "I've read that it's not uncommon for spiritual events to continue to occur with people who have learned how to access another realm."

All this information and remembering had exhausted me. I drove home from the chiropractic office and spent the rest of the afternoon thinking about Jim's words and reliving my buried memories.

Answers Bring More Questions

As I contemplated my near-death experience in the weeks that followed, the way I recalled that day at the creek seemed as real as any other childhood memory. But I couldn't help doubting myself. *Did it really happen? If so, why didn't I know about it?*

Even more than the incidents that led up to the drowning, the memory of leaving my body and going to a heavenly realm and seeing angels, my beloved relatives, and Jesus seemed impossible. I had a lot to ponder.

The memory was so precious that I kept it to myself for a few weeks. The only one I felt safe sharing with was God. *Why wasn't I able to remember until now?* There had to be a reason the Lord was letting me remember what had been hidden from me for so long—almost a lifetime.

After a few weeks, I concluded the Lord put a veil over my memory when I was young so I wouldn't remember. The ordeal would have been too much for a child, and my knowledge of the experience would have surely changed the way I interacted with my family. I was too immature to handle knowing I had a near-death experience, but many questions remained. *Why was I remembering everything now? And why had my family never spoken of the nearly tragic event?*

I couldn't understand how an event so potentially life changing never came up in family conversations over the last forty years. If not with my parents, surely one of my older siblings could have mentioned it.

A Bible verse that I'd memorized from school zigzagged through my thoughts. It was the same one the minister read at Bob's funeral months ago: "For everything there is a season, and a time for every matter under heaven: a time to be born, and a time to die; a time to plant, and a time to pluck up what is planted." (Ecclesiastes 3:1–2, NRSV)

I desperately wanted to know the details that accompanied the scenes I saw in my mind. In order to fully believe my NDE, I needed proof that the events that day at the creek actually happened. I had to make sure my memory was correct.

It was time. Mom and I needed to talk.

Visiting Mom

One Saturday a couple of weeks later, I made the two-hour drive to Cape Girardeau. My mother had recently moved into an independent-living apartment. Daddy had passed on, and there was no reason for her to spend her days cooking, cleaning, or caring for a house as she had done for so many years now that she was living alone.

Mom opened the door wide. "Hi, Linda," she said with a broad grin. "Oh, it's so good to see you!"

I stepped inside. My mother wrapped her arms around me tight, like I was still a child. Her grip had weakened over the years, but her hug still felt so good. I was fortunate to be so loved.

Mom took a whistling pot of water off the stove and made two cups of instant coffee. We sat together at the kitchen table. I made small talk about Gerald and the children. She gave me the latest news about each of my siblings and their families. Then the conversation turned to Bob.

"Joann and the girls are having a rough time without him," said Mom. She looked down and then took a sip of coffee. "I guess we all are."

I put my hand on hers. "It helps me to know he's in a better place now—a much better place."

I nodded my head as we sat quietly for a moment.

"After Bob passed on, he was on my mind a lot. Then I got sick and had to go to the hospital for an operation. Some unexplained things started happening to me when I was there," I said slowly.

Mom knitted her brow. "Is everything okay? Was your operation a success? Tell me what's going on, Linda!"

I put my hand on her shoulder. "Everything's fine, Mom, but something unusual happened right after the surgery."

Mom got real quiet. She put down her coffee cup.

I told her about the sudden pain, being admitted to the hospital, and having the surgery.

"When my operation was over and I got out of the recovery room, I was wheeled to ICU. As I was waking up,

> *"Everything's fine, Mom, but something unusual happened right after the surgery."*

the doctor came to my bedside. He said I was seriously ill. They called my family to come up because they didn't know if I would make it through the night."

Mom's eyes brimmed with tears.

"Don't worry," I said, with a grin. "I made it through okay. I'm here, aren't I?"

Mom took my hand in hers and clasped it to her chest. She was accustomed to my sarcastic sense of humor.

"I'm not sure what happened, but right after the doctor told me I was gravely ill, I lost consciousness. All of a sudden, Bobby's face was close to mine. Even though he'd passed on the week before, he was at my bedside. He told me it wasn't my time."

"Bobby?" The tears that Mom had been trying to hold back ran down her cheeks. I reached over and put my arm around her neck as we cried together. Bob was the first of my siblings to pass on except for Marilyn, my sister who died as a baby.

"I need to ask you something, Mom. Did I almost drown when I was little?"

I saw a box of tissues on an end table. I offered one to Mom and took one for myself. After we had a good cry, I said something I'd been thinking about for a while—ever since I remembered my near-death experience at the creek.

"I loved all three of my brothers, but I always felt a special bond with Bobby," I confided. "I never understood it, but now I think I do."

Mom wiped her eyes as I continued.

"A few weeks after Bob came to my bedside, I started having a recurring scene flash in my mind."

Mom tilted her head with interest.

"I began seeing blond hair floating on top of the water."

I drew in a deep breath. My heart pounded in my chest. "I need to ask you something." I hesitated as I studied her face. "Did I almost drown when I was little?"

Mom's eyes grew wide. She shook her head.

"Oh, Linda, it was horrible!" She got a faraway look in her eyes. "It was the summer of 1952. We were at the church picnic and you fell into the creek. A man pulled you out of the water and gave you CPR. You were so sick—crying and coughing up water."

I knew it! "Why didn't anyone ever talk about it?"

Mom shrugged her shoulders. "I don't know. It was traumatic. You almost died. No one wanted to remember that day; in fact, the church never had a picnic beside a creek again. None of us ever wanted to return there."

I nodded my head. That was thirty-five years ago. It was a different time. People didn't discuss events like that with children in those days.

I took a sip of coffee. "I didn't remember anything that happened that day until recently. Now, I remember it all." I put my elbows on the table. "There's a bit more to the story."

The Rest of the Story

I asked Mom if she had ever heard of a near-death experience.

Mom nodded. "I think so. When someone dies and comes back to life?"

I smiled. "That day at the creek, I went to another realm—it wasn't heaven, but it was near heaven, I think."

I told her about the two angels who tried to comfort me after my soul separated from my body and about being given the choice to return and finish my life on earth.

"I also saw Grandma Reiker!" I exclaimed. "She held me."

A soft smile spread across Mom's face. She reminded me that Grandma had lived with us for a while after I was born. My mother shook her head gently as the long-ago memory surfaced.

I reached across the table and took her hand. I felt the love—the lifetime of love and gratitude I had for my mother and for so many people in our wonderful family.

I explained about being held in the arms of Jesus and seeing colors more beautiful than any rainbow. I described the hues, like a brilliant light that reflected off an icicle and formed a crystal-clear prism. I told her how beautiful and comforting it was in that sacred space. I said I'd decided to stay there because the attraction was so strong—it was just that wonderful.

"But when I hovered above the creek, I saw how panicked and broken-hearted you and Daddy were. Then I saw Bobby. He was beside himself. I could feel his thoughts. He was a wreck. I knew I had to get back in my body. He's what ultimately brought me back."

> *I explained about being held in the arms of Jesus and seeing colors more beautiful than any rainbow.*

Mom nodded.

"You know," Mom said, "I asked Bob to watch over you just before you fell in. He took the whole thing really hard. He was so responsible. He just couldn't forgive himself. That's the main reason we didn't discuss it again. He felt like it was his fault." She shook her head. "If you would have died, I don't think he would have ever gotten over it."

We sat together in silence remembering Bob and missing him too.

The Mysterious Stranger

Your near-death experience is remarkable. You explained that day at the creek just the way I remember it," she said.

Mom sat back in her chair.

"There was something else mysterious that happened that day," she said slowly. "After you started breathing, the man who pulled you out of the water stood up. I quickly bent down and grabbed you up in my arms. You were so tiny. So frightened. We all were."

Mom paused.

"When I looked around to thank that man who saved you, we couldn't find him. No one recognized him or knew who he was. None of us at the picnic ever saw him leave.

"Your daddy and I talked about it. We decided it must have been an angel who pulled you out of that water and saved your life because nobody knew who that mysterious stranger was or where he went."

Holy chills ran down my spine.

"You might be right," I said. "Maybe it was one of the angels in heaven. What if the one who held me when I was in that celestial space followed me? Could he have comforted my spirit when I drowned, then revived my body here on earth?"

"I wouldn't be surprised," Mom said.

Discovering My Purpose

The next few years passed uneventfully. Gerald and I worked. Our children grew up. Life happened, as it is said. But there wasn't a day that went by that I didn't think about my time in the heavenly realm.

I had few people to talk to about my extraordinary experience, so it helped me to write. I kept what I called a "God journal." Sometimes I'd write prayers or ask God questions. Other times I composed poetry.

I knew I had a purpose, a reason I was still on earth, but I wasn't clear what it was. There was no doubt in my mind that God let me choose to stay on earth. If He didn't have a specific purpose for me, I couldn't believe He would allow me to stay when I was confronted with death on two occasions.

I reconnected with a childhood friend—actually, he was one of Bob's friends. We talked about how much we missed my brother, and I felt prompted to share how Bob came to me and told me it wasn't my time when I was in the hospital about five years earlier.

While each NDE is unique, many of us have experienced the same unconditional love and deep compassion.

He leaned in close. "I've had a near-death experience too." He told me about an educational nonprofit organization called the International Association for Near-Death Studies (IANDS). "Come to a meeting with me next month."

The abundance of research and supporting material was fascinating. The organization had been in existence since 1981, but I was just now finding out about it. IANDS' purpose was to promote multidisciplinary exploration of near-death and similar experiences, their effects on people's lives, and their implications for beliefs about life and death.

I joined IANDS and went to a conference. I discovered that while each NDE is unique, many of us have experienced the same components of unconditional love and deep compassion. I wasn't alone. It thrilled me that others were passionate about learning more on this topic.

A Lifetime of Learning

Mom passed on fifteen years after she and I had our visit during which I told her about my NDE. I felt blessed to be at her bedside and to share her last moments on earth before she went to her true home in heaven. I considered it an honor to help my mother transition from this life by letting her know what happens in that heavenly place. Because of my NDE, Mom was not afraid. She was at peace and ready to go home.

I imagine she had a fantastic reunion seeing her loved ones—Daddy, her parents, Bob, and baby Marilyn. I wished I could be with them too. After all, I'd gotten a glimpse of what waited on the other side.

I often think about my childhood NDE and hear Jesus's soft voice encouraging me by saying, "If you go back you will learn many things." He was right. I believe my life here on earth was created in order to learn and to grow my soul into becoming more loving and compassionate.

This time here on earth is also for fulfilling our purpose. Sometimes it takes a long time to figure out one's purpose, but it's part of our contract, the reason we are here.

Now that I'm in my seventies, I wonder if I've learned everything God has in store for me. One thing I know for sure is that love is of the utmost importance. When I was at the creek that Sunday in 1952, Bobby was watching over me. An angel may have pulled me out of the water, but it was love—Bob's love for me and the love I had for him— that truly saved me. That powerful love is eternal. That love never dies.

When my work is done and it's my turn to go home, I look forward to the day when I'll see Mom, Daddy, Bob, Grandma Reiker, and all my loved ones who have passed on before me. I look forward to hearing them say, "Linda, come with us and we will walk you home."

My Life since My Near-Death Experience

Linda Jacquin

I long to be back with God, to see the people who have gone before me, to feel the love of that place. Some people do not believe there is an afterlife, but I have been there, and I know I will see all my loved ones when I go back.

Q What has been the biggest challenge since returning from your NDE?

A Homesickness. The realm where I was is my true home, but I'm so grateful to God that I was given the choice to return. Many people don't get a choice. When it's their time, they must go. Everybody's contract is different. I would not want anybody else's contract. Each one is individual.

Q What do you mean by a contract?

A I look at my contract as what God wants me to do with my life, including sharing the love and acceptance I experienced and to help other experiencers process their NDE. And I think my contract has changed over time based on all of the different aspects of my NDEs.

Sharing my story in this book is part of my contract. I have written poems about my experience and I give them to people who have lost a loved one as a way to comfort them. I also have been interviewed on television and was featured in the film *Cheating Death: Beyond and Back* and was a consultant for the children's book about near-death experiences.

I'm sure that my work with IANDS is also part of my contract. I helped start retreats for near-death experiencers and people who have had spiritually transformative experiences. I met my current husband, Eric, at one of those retreats. I had been divorced for about ten years at the time. I saw this new person across the room, so I went over to introduce myself. It was a divine setup because we married a year later.

Q ***How have your NDEs changed your relationship with God?***

A My NDEs changed how I see God and religion. I used to think I could pick and choose when and how I accessed God—that I needed to be in a church or that there was a specific time and way I should talk to Him. Now I know God is everywhere. I feel Him when I take a walk. I feel God when I see something beautiful in nature, like the stars in the sky. I see God's love and kindness in others. None of us can put God in a box. Being loving and compassionate—that's what God is about.

A Note from the Editors

We hope you enjoyed *A Love beyond Words,* published by Guideposts. For over 75 years, Guideposts, a nonprofit organization, has been driven by a vision of a world filled with hope. We aspire to be the voice of a trusted friend, a friend who makes you feel more hopeful and connected.

By making a purchase from Guideposts, you join our community in touching millions of lives, inspiring them to believe that all things are possible through faith, hope, and prayer. Your continued support allows us to provide uplifting resources to those in need. Whether through our communities, websites, apps, or publications, we inspire our audiences, bring them together, and comfort, uplift, entertain, and guide them.

To learn more, please go to guideposts.org.

We would love to hear from you:

To make a purchase or view our many publications, please go to shopguideposts.org.

To call us, please dial (800) 932-2145

Or write us at Guideposts, P.O. Box 5815, Harlan, Iowa 51593